SHIELDING THE FLAME

AN INTIMATE CONVERSATION WITH DR. MAREK EDELMAN, THE LAST SURVIVING LEADER OF THE WARSAW GHETTO UPRISING

HANNA KRALL

TRANSLATED BY JOANNA STASINSKA AND LAWRENCE WESCHLER

HENRY HOLT AND COMPANY   NEW YORK

Library of Congress Cataloging-in-Publication Data
Krall, Hanna.
Shielding the flame.
Translation of: Zdążyć przed Penem Bogiem.
1. Jews—Poland—Warsaw—Persecutions. 2. Warsaw
(Poland)—History—Uprising of 1943. 3. Holocaust,
Jewish (1939–1945)—Poland—Warsaw. 4. Edelman, Marek,
1921–   . 5. Warsaw (Poland)—Ethnic relations.
I. Edelman, Marek, 1921–   . II. Title.
DS135.P62W277713   1986   940.54'05   85-210
ISBN 0-03-006002-8

First American Edition
Designed by Susan Hood
Printed in the United States of America
1 3 5 7 9 10 8 6 4 2

ISBN 0-03-006002-8

Those people went quietly and with dignity. It is a horrendous thing, when one is going so quietly to one's death. It is infinitely more difficult than to go out shooting.

—Marek Edelman

To the memory of my father,
who went thus,
so quietly to his death.

—Hanna Krall

INTRODUCTION

BY TIMOTHY GARTON ASH

Few peoples in history have lived so closely together as the Jews and the Poles. Few peoples are so far apart today. A hundred years ago, on the eve of the great emigration to the United States, four-fifths of world Jewry could still be found in the area of the old Polish commonwealth, then partitioned among the Russian, German and Austro-Hungarian empires. As late as 1939 the Polish Jewish community was still the largest in Europe, comprising some 10 percent of the population of the pre-war Polish state: more than three million people. Almost all of them perished in the Holocaust. The few who survived, and chose to remain in Poland, played a very significant part in the political and intellectual life of the post-war state, for good and ill. But in 1968 an appalling "anti-Zionist" campaign, orchestrated by powerful factions in the ruling Communist Party and security services, forced most of the remaining Polish Jews to leave their jobs and, finally, the country. In this book, Hanna Krall recalls in passing a desperately poignant scene from the 1970s. An elderly man moves down the line of a funeral procession in Warsaw's Jewish cemetery, patiently asking each mourner, "Excuse me, are you perhaps Jewish?", "Excuse me, are you perhaps . . . ?" He needs ten Jews to recite the Kaddish. He can find only seven in the entire cemetery. The Jewish cemetery.

The gulf between Poles and Jews today is not just a matter of physical separation. There has also been an extraordinary divorce of Polish and Jewish memory. A Polish child growing up in the 1970s learned next to nothing about the immense Jewish part in Polish history, let alone about the Polish part in Jewish history. "Jews" for this Polish child were no more than strange, remote, semi-mythical figures, ritually denounced as "Zionist aggressors" by the communist press (and therefore probably a "Good Thing," since to be denounced by the communists is the surest sign of goodness); surfacing ambiguously in the anecdotes of grandparents (and therefore, on the other hand, perhaps a "Bad Thing"); but really little more familiar than the Ishmaelites and Amalekites who were also to be found misbehaving in the Bible. Certainly he would never have met a Jew: until, perhaps, as a young man he accidentally discovered that his best friend was Jewish.

This divorce of Polish and Jewish memory is absurd when it obscures the centuries of common history up to 1939. It is positively grotesque when it distorts the history of the Nazi occupation, under which both peoples suffered as even they— God knows, no strangers to suffering—had never suffered before. Insofar as any statistics can be relied upon, the dimensions of that suffering are roughly as follows. One in every six citizens of the pre-war Polish Republic perished during the war. This was proportionately the largest loss of any pre-war *state*. It may usefully be compared with the Soviet Union's loss of perhaps one in every nine of its pre-war citizens: the "twenty million dead" who are so often cited as an explanation, and even a moral justification, of the Soviet Union's present oppression of both Poles and Jews. But the proportional loss of the Jewish *nation* was far larger than that of any other—however you choose to define "nation." Of the roughly six million pre-war Polish citizens who died, approximately three million were Jewish, while the other three million were mostly ethnic Poles.

Yet if you took a cross-section of the Polish and Jewish national memories a decade ago what would you have found? It would be no more than a slight exaggeration to say that most Poles remembered those three million martyred Jews only as martyred Poles, while most Jews remembered those three million martyred Poles only as anti-Semites. It was as if each martyrology felt compelled to exclude the other. This was both tragic and ridiculous. A young Pole, brought up to regard his nation as a righteous and heroic victim of history, was shocked by a Jewish indictment that seemed to declare him more guilty than the Nazis. Inspired by the memory of a Home Army resistance fighter—an uncle perhaps, or a family friend—who died in Auschwitz, he was astonished to find that in the West Auschwitz had become an exclusively Jewish symbol. But the Western visitor to Poland could be equally astonished by the distorted official presentation of history there. "Made sick," I find that I noted in my diary when I first visited the State Museum in Oswiecim-Brzezinka (that is, Auschwitz-Birkenau), "made sick by the lies *even here*. . . ." Among the "pavilions of the victim nations" I was amazed to discover a "Pavilion of the German Democratic Republic." East Germany—a victim of the Holocaust! Then I looked for a "Pavilion of Israel." In vain. The plan marked a "Pavilion of the Martyrology of Jews." I went there. It was closed.

Of course this was only one of many areas in which the communist regime falsified history. State-organized lying also covered the murder of Polish officers by Soviet forces at Katyn, the whole resistance record of the noncommunist Home Army, and the role of the Catholic Church. The difference was this. What our schoolboy did not learn about these subjects at school, he was certain to learn—at least in outline—from his own family, from friends, and from the Church. But, with a very few exceptions, these alternative sources of instruction did not perform the same service for knowledge of the history of the Polish Jews. They did not, for example, point out the fundamental difference between the concentration camps (e.g., Auschwitz) and the extermination camps (e.g., Auschwitz-Birkenau).

It was above this gloomy landscape of amnesia, prejudice, and lies that Hanna Krall's extraordinary interview with Marek Edelman exploded like an SOS flare when it first appeared in a literary journal in 1976. Published as a book in 1977, 10,000 copies sold out in just a few days (and another 30,000 in the second printing). And the tremendous response that it elicited from Polish readers showed that all was not as dark as it seemed. A new generation of Poles was not satisfied with what their parents, their state, and their church were telling them—or rather, *not* telling them—about the Jewish part in Polish history. And this was only the beginning. A decade later we find a much less uniformly somber landscape. There were some weeks in 1985 when you could not open a Polish paper without finding yet another article about Polish-Jewish relations. The immediate cause of this outpouring was, admittedly, an external one: Claude Lanzmann's marvelous film *Shoah*, segments of which were shown on Polish television. But the Polish debate about *Shoah* reflected a process of rediscovery that began with books like Hanna Krall's, and for which (as the translators explain in their Afterword) the Solidarity revolution has been a powerful catalyst. As I write, this process is still being carried forward, painfully, unevenly, but insistently, in several interacting worlds of public discourse: in the extraordinarily vigorous unofficial (*"samizdat"*) press, in independent (but legal) Catholic journals like *Znak* and *Wiez*, but also in wholly official papers like the weekly *Polityka,* for which Hanna Krall herself wrote in the years before martial law. Polish-Jewish studies are at long last being introduced at a few Polish universities.

Hand in hand with this general process of national redis-covery there has been a particular, personal, and deeply mov-ing rediscovery, which may be traced back directly to Hanna Krall's book. This is the rediscovery of Marek Edelman, the only surviving leader of the Warsaw Ghetto uprising to re-main in Poland—and his transformation into a national hero. For thirty years after the war, Edelman lived and worked quietly as a cardiologist in Lodz, loved and honored by those who knew him but enjoying no wider fame. The publication of this book gave him a wider fame: and then his passionate involvement in Solidarity lifted him to the status of a national hero. There is something profoundly satisfying, and hope-inspiring, in this secular beatification, suggesting as it does that Poles and Jews might, after all, find their way forward to a common history. Marek Edelman is probably the first Jewish leader ever to become a Polish hero. But there is also something unsettling here. For what gives Edelman's intimate conversation with Hanna Krall its peculiar cutting edge is, in fact, his own agonized *questioning* of precisely that romantic stereotype of "heroism" in which he has now been cast.

"Such honorable men. So heroic. So Polish," a Polish Home Army survivor says of the Warsaw Ghetto insurgents. "They preserved Jewish honor," comments another. And a double number of the excellent Catholic monthly *Znak* devoted to Polish-Jewish affairs carried next to its title page a photograph of three young Ghetto fighters with the dedication "to the memory of those who chose to die with dignity." So the few hundred Ghetto fighters died heroically, with honor and dig-nity. But what, then, of the four hundred thousand who left the Ghetto without offering armed resistance?

By the beginning of 1943 there was only one real question

for those still left inside the Warsaw Ghetto: "How should we die?" Edelman and his friends, most of them barely turned twenty, discussed it: "The majority of us favored an uprising. After all, humanity had agreed that dying with arms was more beautiful than without arms. Therefore we followed this consensus." But was humanity right? Well, one thing is certain, says Edelman now, "It's much *easier* to die shooting [my italics]. Anyway, people have always thought that shooting is the highest form of heroism. So we were shooting." But on the upper floor of his hospital a mother was giving birth, just as the Germans cleared people out of the lower floors, in the "liquidation action." The doctor handed the newborn baby to the nurse, who immediately smothered it with a pillow. The nurse was nineteen years old. "The doctor didn't say a thing to her. Not a word. And this woman knew herself what she was supposed to do." Elsewhere on the upper floor there were several rooms with sick children. As the Germans were entering the ground floor, a woman doctor managed to poison them all. "You see, Hanna," says Edelman, "you don't understand anything. She saved these children from the gas chamber. *People thought she was a hero* [my italics]." So what, then, in that world turned upside down, was heroism? Or honor? Or dignity? And where was God? Edelman's answer to this last question is startling. God, he says, was on the side of the persecutors. A malicious God. Even today, every time he has a heart patient on the operating table, he feels that he is competing with a malicious God to shield the flame of human life. "God is trying to blow out the candle and I'm quickly trying to shield the flame, taking advantage of His brief inattention."

In such passages, *Shielding the Flame* goes far beyond its obvious documentary value as a unique personal record of a unique historical event, and beyond its particular significance as a contribution to Poland's rediscovery of a part of herself.

It becomes a commentary on the human condition. It asks questions of us all. The English-speaking reader may at first be a little baffled by Hanna Krall's style of writing, a kind of Polish "New Journalism," leaping, sometimes breathlessly, and without explanation, from past to present and back again. (As she recently wrote her American translators: "I am afraid of your readers. I feel myself so far from them and from your world. Your world is quite present and happens nowadays. For me 'yesterday' is absolutely mixed together with 'today.' I do not feel any border, either in my writing or in my life. It sounds like an obsession, but it may be normal for somebody who belongs to 1 percent, or even to 3 percent of a people—the Jewish people—who survived in Poland. It is not literature; it may be very real indeed.") All I can say is: please persevere, do read on. The author has good reasons. The point of this mixing will soon become clear. In the end, through all the doubt and questioning, Marek Edelman's story does itself, triumphantly, "show an affirming flame."

SHIELDING THE FLAME

Ihat day you were wearing a sweater made of red, fluffy wool. "It was a beautiful sweater, made of angora. From a very rich Jew . . ." Two leather belts crisscrossed the sweater, and in the middle, atop your chest, a flashlight. "Hanna, I wish you could have seen me then!" you told me when I asked about that day, April 19th . . .

—Is that what I said? It was cold. In April, the nights are cold, especially for those who haven't been eating much. So I put the sweater on. It's true, I found it among some things that belonged to this Jew: one day they pulled his whole family out of their basement, and I took an angora sweater. It was top quality. That guy had loads of money: before the war he'd donated a plane or tank or something like that to the Fund for National Defense.

I know you like that sort of thing. That's probably why I mentioned it.

—Oh, no. You mentioned it because you wanted to show me something. The matter-of-factness and the calm. That's what you were trying to demonstrate.

—I simply talk about it the way we all spoke about it at the time.

—Well, the sweater, the crossing belts . . .

—Write also two guns. The guns completed the outfit, very

1

de rigueur. You figured in those days that if you had two guns, you had everything.

—April 19th: you were awakened by shooting, you got dressed . . .

—No, not yet. The shooting woke me up, true, but it was cold, and besides, the shooting was far away, and there was no reason to get up.

I got dressed around noon.

There was one guy with us who had smuggled in arms from the Aryan side. He was supposed to have headed back immediately, but it was already too late. When they started shooting, he told me that he had a daughter in Zamosc in a convent and that he knew he would not survive, but that I would, so that after the war I was supposed to take care of this daughter. I said: "All right, all right, stop talking nonsense."

—Well?

—Well what?

—Did you manage to find this daughter?

—Yes, I did. . . .

—Listen, we agreed that you would talk, right? It is April 19th. They have started shooting. You've gotten dressed. This guy from the Aryan side is talking about his daughter. What next?

—We went out to look around. We crossed the courtyard—there were a few Germans there. Actually, we should have killed them, but we hadn't had practice in killing yet, and besides, we were still a little afraid, so we didn't kill them.

After about three hours the shooting died down.

It got silent.

Our area was the so-called Brush Factory Ghetto—Franciszkanska, Swietojerska, Bonifraterska streets.

2

We had mined the factory gate.

The next day, when the Germans approached, we plunged the plug in, and about a hundred of them got wiped out. I don't remember exactly, you'd have to look it up somewhere. Actually, I remember less and less. About any of my patients, I could tell you ten times more.

After the mine's explosion, they started charging at us in an extended line. We loved it. Forty of us, a hundred of them, a whole column, in full battle array, crawling along. It was obvious that now they were taking us seriously.

Before the day had ended, they sent over three men with their guns held down, carrying white sashes. They called out that if we'd agree to a ceasefire, they would send us to a special camp. We shot at them. I later found that scene in Stroop's reports: them, parliamentarians with a white banner—us, bandits, opening fire. By the way, we missed, but it doesn't matter.

—How come it doesn't matter?

—The important thing was just that we were shooting. We had to show it. Not to the Germans. They knew better than us how to shoot. We had to show it to this other, the non-German world. People have always thought that shooting is the highest form of heroism. So we were shooting.

—Why did you choose that very day, April 19th?

—We didn't choose it. The Germans chose it. That was the day the liquidation of the Ghetto was scheduled to begin. There were phone calls from the Aryan side—that they were getting everything ready, that the walls were being surrounded on the outside. On the night of the 18th we met at Anielewicz's, all five of us, the whole command staff. I was probably the oldest one there, twenty-two years old; Anielewicz was a year younger. Together, all five of us, we were a hundred and ten years old.

There wasn't much to talk about by that time anymore. "Well?" "Have they called from the city?" Anielewicz takes the central Ghetto, his deputies—Geller and myself—we divvy up Toebbens' Sheds and the Brush Factory. "See you tomorrow." We did say good-bye to each other, the only thing we had never done before.

—Why was it Anielewicz who became your commander?

—He very much wanted to be a commander, so we chose him. He was a little childlike in this ambition, but he was a talented guy, well read, full of energy. Before the war he'd lived on Solec Street. His mother sold fish. When she had any left over, she would have him buy red paint and paint the gills so the fish would look fresh. He was constantly hungry. When he first came back to the Ghetto from Silesia and we gave him something to eat, he would shield the plate with his hand, so that nobody could take anything away from him.

He had a lot of youthful verve and enthusiasm, only he had never before seen an "action." He hadn't seen the people being loaded into trains at the Umschlagplatz. And such a thing—when you see four hundred thousand people being sent off to gas chambers—can break a person.

We did not meet on April 19th. I saw him the day after. He was already a different man. Celina told me: "You know, it happened to him yesterday. He was just sitting and muttering: 'We're all going to die. . . .' " He managed to get roused up again only once after that. We got a message from the Home Army* to wait in the northern part of the Ghetto. We didn't know exactly what it was all about, and in the end, it didn't work out anyway: the guy who went there to check it out got burned alive in Mila Street, we could hear him screaming all day. . . . Do you think that can impress anybody any-

*The Home Army, the principal and largest clandestine anti-Nazi armed organization in Poland.

more—one burning guy after four hundred thousand burned people?

—I think that one burned guy makes a bigger impression than four hundred thousand, and four hundred thousand a bigger impression than six million. So, you didn't know exactly what this message was about . . .

—He must have thought that some reinforcements were being sent. We kept trying to dissuade him: "Let it go, the area there is completely dead, we won't get through."

You know what?

I think that all along he had actually convinced himself of the possibility of some sort of victory.

Obviously, he never spoke about it before. On the contrary. "We are going to die," he would yell, "there is no way out, we'll die for our honor, for history. . . ." All the sorts of things one says in such cases. But today I think that all the time he maintained some kind of a childlike hope.

He had a girlfriend. Pretty, blond, warm. Her name was Mira. On May 7th he came with her to our place in Franciszkanska Street.

On May 8th he shot her first and then himself. Jurek Wilner had apparently declared: "Let's all die together." Lutek Rotblat shot his mother and sister, then everybody started shooting. By the time we managed to get back there, there were only a few people left alive; eighty people had committed suicide. "This is how it should have been," we were told later. "The nation has died, its soldiers have died. A symbolic death." You, too, probably like such symbols?

There was a young woman with them, Ruth. She shot herself seven times before she finally made it. She was such a pretty, tall girl with a peachy complexion, but she wasted six bullets.

There is a park now at that place, with a landmark, a rock, an inscription. When the weather turns nice, mothers with kids go there, and in the evenings young guys go there with their girls. It is actually a collective grave; we never dug the bones out.

—You had forty soldiers. Did it ever occur to you to do the same thing?

—Never. They should never have done it. Even though it was a very good symbol. You don't sacrifice a life for a symbol. I did not have any doubts about that—at least not during those twenty days. I was capable of bashing somebody in the face myself if they started to get hysterical. In general, I was able to do a lot of things then. To lose five men in a battle and not feel guilty. To nod off to sleep while the Germans were drilling holes in order to blow us up (I simply knew that there was nothing more to be done at the moment); and only when they'd break for lunch at noon, we'd quickly do whatever was necessary to get out. (I wasn't nervous—perhaps because actually nothing could happen. Nothing greater than death. It was always death that was at stake, not life. You see, maybe there was no drama at all there. Drama is when you can make a decision, when something depends on you, whereas there, everything had been predetermined. Nowadays, in the hospital, there it's life that's at stake—and each time I have to make a decision now, I get much more nervous.)

And I was capable of one other thing there. I was capable of telling a guy who'd asked me to give him the address of a contact on the Aryan side: "Not yet, it's too early." His name was Stasiek . . . you see, I can't remember last names. "Marek," he said, "there must be some place *over there* I can get to. . . ." Was I supposed to tell him that there was no such place? So I told him: "It is too early yet."

—Was it possible to see anything beyond the wall on the Aryan side?

—Oh yes. The wall only reached the second floor. And

6

already from the third floor one could see the *other* street. We could see a merry-go-round, people, we could hear music, and we were terribly afraid that this music would drown us out and that those people would never notice a thing, that nobody in the world would notice a thing: us, the struggle, the dead. . . . That this wall was so huge, that nothing, no message about us, would ever make it out.

But we later heard from London that General Sikorski posthumously awarded the Virtuti Militari Cross to Michal Klepfisz. The guy in our attic who managed to cover over that machine gun with his body, so that we could get through.

An engineer, in his twenties. An exceptionally good guy.

Thanks to him we forced back one attack—and a bit after that those three men with their white rosettes arrived. The parliamentarians.

I would stand in this place. Exactly here. Only the gate was wooden then. This cement post is the same, that barrack, and probably even those poplars.

Wait, why actually did I always stand on this side?

Oh, I see, because the crowd would march on by the other side. I was probably afraid that they would rake me in, too.

By that time I was working as a messenger at the hospital, and this was my job: to stand by the gate at the Umschlagplatz and select out "sick" people. Our people would pick out those who should be saved, and I would select them out as "sick."

I was merciless. One woman begged me to pull out her fourteen-year-old daughter, but I was only able to take one more person and I took Zosia, who was our best courier. I selected her out four times and each time ended up having to take her out all over again.

At the beginning it was the people without life tickets who were being paraded past me. The Germans had issued these tickets, and those who got them were promised survival. In those days everybody in the Ghetto had only one goal: to get a ticket. But later, they were even taking out those with the tickets.

Still later it was announced that the right to live was being reserved for employees of factories. Sewing machines were necessary in these factories, so people began thinking that sewing machines might save their lives and they were ready to pay any price for a sewing machine. But afterward, they started taking away even those with the machines.

Finally, they announced that they would distribute bread. That everybody who volunteered for hard labor would get three kilograms of bread and jam.

Listen, my dear. Do you have any idea what bread meant at that time in the Ghetto? Because if you don't, you will never understand how thousands of people could voluntarily come for the bread and go on with this bread to the camp at Treblinka. Nobody has understood it thus far.

They were giving out that bread right here, in this very place. Oblong, browned loaves of rye bread.

And you know what?

Those people would go, in order, by fours, to get this bread, and then right onto the train car. There were so many such volunteers that they had to wait in line! It was required that they send two trains a day to Treblinka—and still, there was not enough space for all those who were willing to go.

Yes, we knew.

In 1942 we'd sent a friend, Zygmunt, to find out what was going on with those trains. He'd gone with the railway workers. In Sokolow they'd told him that at that point the railroad divided in two, and that one sidetrack went to Treblinka. Every day a freight train loaded with people would pass that way and return empty; but food supplies were never sent there.

Zygmunt came back to the Ghetto, we wrote about it in

our newspaper—and nobody believed it. "Have you gone insane?" people would say when we were trying to convince them that they were not being taken to work. "Would they be sending us to death with bread? So much bread would be wasted!"

The action lasted from July 22nd till September 8th, 1942—six weeks. During those six weeks I stood by the gate. Here, at this spot. I saw four hundred thousand people off from this square. I was looking at the same cement post you are looking at now.

In the building of that vocational school over there, that was our hospital. They liquidated it on September 8th, the last day of the action. On the upper floor there were a few rooms with children. As the Germans were entering the ground floor, a woman doctor managed to poison the kids.

You see, Hanna, you don't understand anything. She saved these children from the gas chamber. People thought she was a hero.

In this hospital, sick people were lying on the floor waiting to be loaded onto the train cars, and the nurses were searching out their parents in the crowd and injecting them with poison. They saved this poison for their closest relatives. And she, this doctor, had given *her own* cyanide to kids who were complete strangers!

There was only one man who could have declared the truth out loud: Czerniakow. They would have believed him. But he had committed suicide.

That wasn't right: one should die with a bang. At that time this bang was most needed—one should die only after having called other people into the struggle.

Actually, this is the only thing we reproach him for.

—"We"?

—Me and my friends. The dead ones. We reproach him for having made his death his own private business.

We were convinced that it was necessary to die publicly, under the world's eyes.

We had several ideas. Dawid said that we should jump the walls—everybody, all those still alive in the Ghetto—force our way over to the Aryan side, and dig in along the inclined dikes of the Citadel, in rows, one above the other, and wait there until the Gestapo surrounded us with machine guns and shot us all, row by row.

Estera wanted to set fire to the Ghetto so that we would all burn in it. "Let the wind spread our ashes," she would say. At that time, that did not sound grandiloquent, just objective.

The majority of us favored an uprising. After all, humanity had agreed that dying with arms was more beautiful than without arms. Therefore we followed this consensus. In the Jewish Combat Organization there were only two hundred twenty of us left. Can you even call that an uprising? All it was about, finally, was that we not just let them slaughter us when our turn came.

It was only a choice as to the manner of dying.

That interview was translated into several foreign languages and angered many people. Mr. S., a writer, wrote to Edelman from the United States that he had had to defend him; he'd written three long articles to calm everyone down and the title had been "The Confession of the Last Living Commander of the Warsaw Ghetto."

People had sent letters to the editors about the interview— in French, English, Yiddish, and in some other European languages—that he had stripped everything of its magnitude, but basically it was about the fish. The fish whose gills Anielewicz used to paint red so that his mother in Solec Street could sell yesterday's merchandise.

Anielewicz, a peddler's son, painting fish gills red—that beat all! So that this writer, Mr. S., did not have an easy job. But there was also a certain German from Stuttgart who wrote a nice letter.

"*Sehr geehrter Herr Doktor*," wrote that German, who during the war had spent time in the Warsaw Ghetto as a Wehrmacht soldier. "I saw there bodies of dead people lying in the streets, many bodies, covered with paper. I remember, it was horrible. We are both victims of that terrible war. Could you please drop me a few words?"

Obviously, he wrote the guy back, that he was pleased to have heard from him and fully understood the feelings of a young German soldier who for the first time saw bodies covered with paper.

This story about the writer, Mr. S., reminded Edelman of his trip to America in 1963. He was flown there for a meeting with union leaders. He remembers there was a table with some twenty gentlemen sitting around it. Their faces expressed concentration and emotion: these were the presidents of the trade unions that during the war had given money for arms for the Ghetto.

The chairman greets him and the discussion starts. What is human memory and is it proper to build monuments or maybe buildings—that sort of literary dilemma. Edelman was being very careful not to just blab out something improper, such as, for instance, "And what importance does any of it have today?" He had no right to harm them in this way. "Be careful," he kept saying to himself, "careful, they have tears in their eyes. They gave money for arms. They went to President Roosevelt to ask him if they were true, all these stories about the Ghetto. You have to be good to them."

(They must have gone to Roosevelt after one of the first reports prepared by "Waclaw," shortly after Tosia Goliborska ransomed him from the Gestapo with her Persian carpet. The report was smuggled out by a messenger in his tooth, inside a filling, on microfilm, and reached the United States via London. But they'd had a hard time crediting those thousands of people allegedly processed into soap and those thousands driven through the Umschlagplatz, so they'd gone to their president to ask if these things could be taken seriously.)

So he *was* good to them. He let them be moved and talk about human memory. But then, unintentionally, he hurt them so terribly: "Do you really think that it can be called an uprising?"

Coming back to the fish. In the French translation of the interview published in the weekly magazine *L'Express*, they were not fish but *du poisson*, and Anielewicz's mother, that Jewish peddler from Solec Street, would buy *un petit pot de peinture rouge*. Well—can one still take him seriously, this Anielewicz who puts *peinture rouge* on gills (*les ouïes*); is he still Anielewicz?

It is like attempting to tell one's cousins in England the story of their grandmother who was dying of hunger during the Ghetto uprising. Just before she died, the religious old lady had asked for something to eat. "Doesn't matter," she'd said, "it doesn't have to be kosher, it can even be a *kotlet wieprzowy*."

But one has to tell the story in English to one's English cousins, so in English, Grandma was asking not for a *kotlet wieprzowy* but for a *pork chop*, and at that moment she simply stops being that dying grandmother. It becomes possible to talk about her without hysteria, calmly, the way one might tell an interesting story at a civilized English dinner.

They insist that this couldn't be the real Anielewicz, this one with *peinture rouge*. And there must be some truth to that, since so many people insist on it. They write that one mustn't say such things about the Commander.

—Listen, Hanna, Edelman says, from now on we'll have to be careful. We'll choose our words carefully.

Of course, we shall.
We'll choose our words very thoughtfully. And we'll try not to hurt anybody.
One morning the American writer, Mr. S., calls. He is in Warsaw. He has seen Antek and Celina, and he wants to talk about it in person.
Well—this is serious business. Because one can neglect what everybody in the world says about these things, but there are two people whose opinions can't be ignored and those people are precisely Celina and Antek. Antek, Anielewicz's deputy and the representative of the ZOB (the Jewish Combat Organization) on the Aryan side, who had left the Ghetto shortly before the beginning of the uprising, and Celina, who was with them in the Ghetto all the time, from the first day till the evacuation through the sewers.
Antek has kept silent all this time. And here, Mr. S. arrives and says he's just seen Antek a week earlier.
I have a feeling that Edelman is a little nervous. For no reason, as it turns out. Mr. S. says that Antek reassures Edelman about his friendship and respect for him, and approves, except for a few details, of the entire interview.
"What details?" I ask Mr. S.
Antek has said, for instance, that there were not two hundred of them in the uprising, there were more: five hundred, maybe even six hundred of them.

(—Antek says there were six hundred of you. Shall we change this figure?

13

—No, Edelman says, there were two hundred and twenty of us.

—But Antek wants, Mr. S. wants, everybody wants you to be at least a little more . . . Shouldn't we just change it?

—After all, it doesn't matter, he says angrily. Can't all of you understand that none of it matters anymore?!)

Oh, and one more thing. Obviously: the fish problem.

It wasn't Anielewicz who painted them, it was his mother. "Write it down, Ms. Krall," says Mr. S., the writer. "That is *very* important."

I return to the problem of choosing words carefully.

Three days after Edelman's departure from the Ghetto, Celemenski arrived and took him to a clandestine meeting with representatives from the underground political parties who wanted to hear a report about the Ghetto uprising. He was the only surviving member of the uprising command and the commander's deputy, so he delivered a report: during those twenty days, he said, it might have been possible to have killed more Germans and to have saved more of our people. But, he said, they had not been properly trained and weren't able to conduct a proper battle. Besides, he said, the Germans also knew how to fight.

Those people looked on at him in total silence, until finally one of them said: "We must try to understand him. He is not a normal man. He is a human wreck."

Because, as it turned out, he was not talking the way he was supposed to talk.

"And how is one supposed to talk?" he asked.

One is supposed to talk with hatred, grandiloquence—one is supposed to scream. There's no other way to express all this except by screaming.

So, from the very beginning, he was no good at talking

about it because he was unable to scream. He was no good as a hero because he lacked grandiloquence.

What bad luck.

The one, the only one, who'd survived was no good as a hero.

Having understood that, he tactfully lapsed into silence. He was silent for quite a long time, for thirty years in fact, and when he finally spoke, it immediately became clear that it would have been better for everybody if he had simply never broken his silence.

He had taken a streetcar to that meeting with the representatives of the various parties. For the first time since leaving the Ghetto he was riding a streetcar, and a horrible thing suddenly happened to him. He was seized by the wish not to have a face. Not because he was afraid that someone would notice him and denounce him; no, he suddenly felt that he had a repugnant, sinister face. The face from the poster "JEWS—LICE—TYPHUS." Whereas everybody else around him had fair faces. They were handsome, relaxed. They could be relaxed because they were aware of their fairness and beauty.

He got off in the Zoliborz district, in an area of little houses. The street was empty and only one elderly woman was watering flowers in her garden. She looked at him from behind her garden's wire netting, and he tried almost not to exist, to take up as little room as possible in that sunny space.

Today, they showed Krystyna Krahelska on TV. Her hair was also fair. She was once Nitschowa's model for the statue of the mermaid which has become a symbol of Warsaw, she used to write poetry, she sang *dumky* (those Ukrainian folk songs), and she was killed during the 1944 Warsaw uprising among the sunflowers.

Some lady was telling Krahelska's story: how she'd been running through some gardens, but that she was so tall that even when bending she'd been unable to hide among those sunflowers.

So, it is a warm August day. She has tied this long, blond hair behind her. She has already written the underground anthem, "Hey, Boys, Affix Your Bayonets!", she's dressed somebody's wound, and now she is running in the sun.

What a beautiful life and a beautiful death! This is the only way a person should die. But this is the way beautiful and fair people live and die. The dark and ugly ones die in an unattractive way: in fear and darkness.

(One could perhaps have hidden at the place of this lady who's telling Krahelska's story. She's not wearing makeup, she certainly hasn't been to the hairdresser and, although you cannot see this on TV, she is probably too wide in the hips, and she hikes in the mountains with a sweater tied round her waist. Her husband wouldn't even have to know that she was hiding somebody, one would only have to be careful not to use the bathroom in the afternoon, between 3:30 and 4 P.M. He has a very regular stomach and uses the bathroom the moment he comes home, even before supper.)

The dark and ugly ones, sapped by hunger, between humid sheets, wait for someone to bring them oats cooked with water or perhaps something from the garbage can. Everything there is gray: faces, hair, sheets. The acetylene lamp is only used sparingly. In the streets, their children tear packages right out of pedestrians' hands in the hope that they might find bread within; they devour everything immediately. In the hospital, children swollen with hunger receive half a powdered egg and one vitamin C tablet each day—this has to be distributed by the physicians because the ward attendant, who is also swollen, cannot handle the torture of the distribution. (Only the doctors and the nurses get food rations: 500 grams of soup and 60 grams of bread. At a special meeting it is decided to sacrifice 200 grams of soup and 20 grams of bread and divide it among the stokers and the ward attendants. Thus, everybody is getting the same: 300 grams of soup and 40 grams of bread per person.) At 18 Krochmalna Street a thirty-year-old woman, Rywka Urman, chewed off a piece of her child, Berek Urman, twelve years old, who had died of starvation the day before. People surrounded her in the court-yard in complete silence, without saying a word. She had gray, tousled hair, a gray face, and crazy eyes. Later, the police came and wrote it all down for the record. At 14 Krochmalna Street a child's body was found in decay. It had been abandoned by its mother, Chudesa Borensztajn, apartment #67. The child's name was Moszek. (The car from the Eternity Mortuary took the corpse away, and Borensztajn explained that she had abandoned it in the street because the community council didn't bury without payment, and besides, she would soon die herself.) People are being taken to the public baths for delousing. On Spokojna Street, they have already been waiting for a day and a night in front of the bath building, and when only enough soup is brought to feed the children, police have to be called to drive the crowd away because people are trying to take food away from the children.

Death by starvation is as unaesthetical as is the hungry life. "Some people fell asleep with a bite of bread in their mouth or during any sort of physical strain, for instance, while running, trying to get some bread."

This comes from a scientific paper.

Doctors in the Ghetto conducted research on hunger because the exact mechanism of death by inanition was at that time unclear from the medical point of view and it seemed wise to take advantage of the occasion. It was an extraordinary occasion. "Never before," the doctors wrote, "has medicine had such rich research material."

17

Still today, it continues to be an interesting problem for physicians.

"For instance," says Dr. Edelman, "the problem of upsetting the balance between water and albumin in a human body. Did they write there anything about electrolytes?" he asks. "Together with water, potassium and salt seep into the connective tissue. See whether they found out anything about the role of albumin."

No, they don't say anything about electrolytes. They note their disappointment that they had been unable to explain anything about this problem that is so interesting from a doctor's point of view—the mechanism of edema in hunger.

Perhaps they would have discovered the role of albumin if they hadn't suddenly had to stop their work, but, unfortunately, they had had to stop it, for which they excuse themselves in the introduction. They were unable to continue the research because "the scientific stock—the human material—was presently annihilated." The liquidation of the Ghetto had begun.

Shortly after the scientific material was annihilated, the researchers were also killed.

Only one of them is still alive: Dr. Teodozja Goliborska. She was investigating basal metabolism in hungry people.

She writes me from Australia that she had known from her readings that the basal metabolism in starving people was slower, but she hadn't suspected that it would prove so much slower, and that this was related to the lower number of breaths and their reduced depth, and in turn the smaller amount of oxygen used by a body in the state of inanition.

(I ask Dr. Goliborska whether later, as a physician, she ever had occasion to make any use of that research. She writes that no, all the people she has treated in Australia have been well fed, indeed some of them overfed.)

Here are some of the results of the research, presented in the paper "Starvation Sickness. Clinical Research Conducted in the Warsaw Ghetto in 1942."

There are three stages of emaciation: Stage I occurs as the excess of fat tissue is being used up. People look younger than usual at this stage. "In the pre-war period we would often find these symptoms in patients who had returned from the spas at Karlsbad, Vichy, etc." Almost all cases studied by the group belonged to Stage II. The exceptions were the cases of Stage III, that is, starvation decrepitude, which in most cases constituted the premortal phase.

Let's proceed to a description of changes in particular organs and systems.

Weight was usually between 30 and 40 kilograms, and it was about 20 to 25 percent lower than pre-war weight. The lowest weight registered was 24 kilograms in a thirty-year-old woman.

Skin is pale, sometimes pale purple.

Nails, especially fingernails, are clawlike . . .

(Perhaps we are discussing all of this at too great length and in too great detail, but this is because it is vital to understand the difference between a beautiful life and an unaesthetical life, and between a beautiful death and an unaesthetical one. It is important. Everything that happened later—everything that happened on April 19th, 1943—was a yearning for a beautiful dying.)

At the beginning, edemas are observed on the face in the eyelid area, on feet, and in some people even edemas of the whole cutaneous integument. If punctured, liquid comes out of subcutaneous tissue. In early fall, a tendency toward frostbite of the fingers and toes can be observed.

Faces are expressionless, masklike.

Thick hair growth can be observed all over the body, especially in women, on faces, in the form of mustaches and whiskers, and sometimes hairiness of the eyelids. In addition, long eyelashes are observed . . .

The mental state is characterized by a paucity of thoughts.

Active and energetic people become apathetic and lethargic. They are sleepy almost all the time. They seem to forget about their hunger, are unaware of its existence, although upon seeing bread, sweets, or meat, they suddenly become aggressive; they will try to devour it even at the risk of exposing themselves to beatings, which they are unable to avoid by running away.

The transition from life to death is slow, almost imperceptible. Death is similar, physiologically, to death in old age.

Autopsy material (3282 complete autopsies were included in the study):

Pigmentation in people who died of starvation: pale or cadaverous pale in 82.5 percent of cases, dark or russet in 17 percent.

There were edemas in one-third of all the bodies submitted to autopsy, in most cases on the lower limbs. The torso and upper limbs were swollen in fewer cases. In most cases edemas were observed in individuals with pale pigmentation. It can be concluded that pale pigmentation appears together with edemas, and russet pigmentation accompanies dry prostration.

Excerpts from an autopsy record (L. rec. aut. 8613):

"Woman, 16 years old. Diagnosis: *Inanitio permagna*. Nutrition very squalid. Brain 1300 grams, very soft, swollen. About 2 liters of clear, yellowish liquid in the abdominal cavity. Heart—smaller than the fist of the corpse."

Frequency of atrophy of particular organs:

In general, the heart, liver, kidneys, and pancreas deteriorate.

Heart atrophy was observed in 82 percent of cases, liver

atrophy in 83 percent, atrophy of pancreas and kidneys in 87 percent. In addition, bones deteriorate—they soften and become spongy.

Livers shrink the most—from about 2 kilograms in a healthy person to 54 grams.

The lowest heart weight was 110 grams.

Only the brain seems virtually not to diminish; it still weighs about 1300 grams.

During the same period the Professor had been working as a surgeon in Radom, in the Saint Casimir Hospital. (The Professor is a tall, grayish, refined man. He has beautiful hands. He likes music, used to play the violin himself. He speaks several foreign languages. His great-grandfather was a Napoleonic officer, his grandfather participated in an anti-Russian rebellion.)

Every day some newly injured partisans would be brought to this hospital.

The partisans usually had belly wounds. It was difficult to get the ones with head injuries to the hospital on time. So he tended to operate on stomachs, spleens, bladders, and large intestines; he was capable of operating on thirty, forty bellies a day.

In summer 1944 they started bringing in thorax cases, because the Warka bridgehead had been created. Many thoraxes were being brought, some mangled by shrapnel or by grenade fragments, or with a bullet-shattered window frame thrust into the chest. Hearts and lungs were sticking out of chest cavities, so it was necessary to repair them somehow and then shove them back into their place.

Once the January offensive started, heads were added: the

Red Army had better transportation than the partisans and now the wounded arrived on time.

"A surgeon has to exercise his fingers all the time," says the Professor. "Like a pianist. I had early and extensive practice."

War is an excellent school for a young surgeon: so the Professor achieved amazing skill in operating on bellies (thanks to the partisans), in operating on heads (thanks to the advancing front), but the Warka bridgehead turned out to provide the most important experience. For during the time of the Warka bridgehead, the Professor for the first time saw an open, beating heart.

Before the war, nobody had ever seen a heart beat. Maybe in an animal, but even this not too often, because there would have been no sense in maltreating an animal so badly, especially since it would have been of no use to medicine anyway. It wasn't until 1947 that for the first time in Poland a thorax was surgically opened. This was done by a Professor Crafoord, who'd come from Stockholm especially for the occasion, but even he hadn't opened up the pericardium. Everybody stood looking as if bewitched at the pericardium as it rhythmically moved, as if there were some small living animal hidden inside. And the Professor was the only one—for not even Professor Crafoord knew—the only one who knew exactly what this thing moving restlessly inside would look like. Because only he—and not the world-famous Swedish guest—had pulled out from the hearts of peasants pieces of rug, splinters, and window frames. It was thanks to this that just five years later, on June 20, 1952, he was able to open the heart of a certain Kwapisz Genowefa and operate on her mitral stenosis.

There is a close and logical relation between those hearts from the Warka area and all the others on which he would later operate, including, of course, also the heart of Mr. Rudny, the haberdashery machine specialist, and that of Mrs. Bubner (whose late husband was very active in the Jewish community, thanks to which she was quite relaxed before the operation, had even been calming the doctors down: "Please, don't worry," she'd told them; "my husband has a very good relationship with God, he will certainly arrange things here so that everything turns out quite all right."), and that of Mr. Rzewuski, president of the Automobile Club—those and many, many other hearts.

Rudny had to have a vein transplanted from his leg into his heart so as to create a wider passage for his blood at a moment just before a heart attack was otherwise about to start. Rzewuski required such a transplant when his heart attack had already started. Mrs. Bubner had to have her blood circulation changed. . . .

Is the Professor scared before such operations?

Oh, yes. He is very scared. He feels fear right here, here, in the belly.

Each time he hopes that at the last moment something will happen that will render it all impossible: the internists will forbid it, the patient will change his mind, maybe even he himself will run out from his office. . . .

What is the Professor so afraid of? God?

Oh, yes, certainly he is very scared of God, but that's not the worst.

Is he scared that the patient may die?

That too, but he knows—everybody knows—that without the operation the patient would die anyway, this is for sure.

So what is he afraid of?

He is afraid that his colleagues will say: *he is making experiments on human beings*. This is the most horrible of all the accusations that can be made.

Doctors have their own board of control regarding professional conduct, and the Professor relates how one day a certain surgeon hit a child with his car. He carried the child into his car, brought him to his hospital ward, cared for him, and cured him. The kid ended up fine, the mother didn't claim anything; only the professional board ruled that caring for this kid in his own hospital ward like that was against medical ethics and rebuked the doctor. He was thereafter unable to exercise his profession, and he soon died of heart disease.

The Professor tells this story just like that, for no particular reason. Because I asked him what a doctor is afraid of.

With these ethics, it becomes much more complicated than one would have thought.

For example: If he had not operated on President Rzewuski's heart, Rzewuski would certainly have died. Nothing special would have happened: dozens of people die during a heart attack. . . . Everybody would have understood, no explanations would have been needed.

However, if they performed the operation and *then* Rzewuski died—oh, that would be quite a different story. Someone might point out that, after all, nobody else in the world was even attempting such interventions. Somebody else might have asked if the Professor was not being too reckless sometimes, and that could already begin to sound like a general accusation . . .

So that now we might begin to imagine what the Professor is thinking of as he sits in his office before an intervention— before this particular intervention—and there, in the operating room, the anesthesiologist is beginning to bustle about, preparing Rzewuski.

Because the Professor has been sitting in his office for quite a while now, even though, if truth be told, it is not at all clear if this is because of Rzewuski. In the operating room they might just as well be bustling about Rudny or Mrs. Bubner. But it has to be admitted that the Professor was the most nervous before Rzewuski.

Because the Professor very much dislikes operating on the hearts of intellectuals. Intellectuals think too much before an operation, their imaginations are too vivid, they're constantly asking themselves and everybody else too many questions, and all this later reflects undesirably in the pulse rate, in the blood pressure, and in the entire process of the operation. A man like Rudny, by contrast, consigns himself into his surgeon's hands with much greater confidence, he does not ask the unnecessary questions, and therefore it is much easier to operate on him.

Thus, let it be Rzewuski, and let the Professor be sitting in his office before the operation that he is going to perform on this intellectual, whose heart is in a state of acute heart attack and who just a few hours before was rushed here from a Warsaw hospital in an emergency ambulance.

The Professor is absolutely alone.

Nearby, just beyond the door, Dr. Edelman is sitting, smoking cigarettes.

What is the problem?

The problem is that it's precisely Edelman who has insisted that Mr. Rzewuski can be operated on during his heart attack; if it were not for this, the whole issue would not have even come up.

For that matter, Mr. Rudny would not have existed either. The Professor had operated on him as the heart attack was just about to begin, and all the manuals of heart surgery declare that this is precisely the state in which a patient mustn't be operated on.

For that matter, there would not have been any idea of reversing Mrs. Bubner's blood flow (and perhaps there wouldn't be Mrs. Bubner herself anymore; this thought, however, doesn't strictly belong with these considerations).

Since the scene in the Professor's office for us, after all, is a mere pretext, we can leave him for a moment at that desk and explain what is actually at stake here with the blood-flow system.

Namely, during one such operation, earlier, an assistant doctor had questioned whether the Professor had taken up an artery or rather a vein—it happens sometimes that blood vessels look similar. Everybody had insisted that it was okay, that it was an artery, but the assistant had persisted: "It is definitely a vein." After coming home, Edelman, who had been at this operation, began to think what actually would have happened had it really been a vein. He began to draw out a sketch on a piece of paper: the oxygenated blood, which, as we know from school, in the pulmonary circulation flows in arteries, could be directed from the main artery directly to the veins—these are still pliable because they haven't been attacked by sclerosis, therefore they would not provoke a heart attack. This blood would flow away through . . .

Edelman is still not quite sure where this blood would flow away, but the next day he shows his sketch to the Professor. The Professor gives it a glance. "It is possible, Professor, right here, and the muscle would be supplied with blood . . . ," Edelman says, and the Professor nods politely. "Oh yes," he says, "that's very interesting," because what, except politeness, can you show someone who suggests that blood can arrive at the heart not through veins but rather through arteries?

Edelman goes back to his hospital and the Professor, back at his house, at night, places the sketch on a little night table next to his bed. The Professor always sleeps with the light on, so as to be able to pull himself together quickly in case he awakens during the night. So this time he also leaves his lamp on, and when, after four hours, he wakes up, he immediately reaches for the piece of paper with Edelman's drawing.

26

It is difficult to state at which moment the Professor stops staring at the drawing and begins to sketch something himself on another piece of paper (he is drawing a bridge linking the main artery with veins), but the fact is that one day he suddenly asks Edelman: "Well, and what is gonna happen with this used blood, if the vein assumes the role of the artery?"

Edelman and Dr. Elzbieta Chetkowska reply that a certain lady, Ratajczak-Pakalska, is working on her Ph.D. on the anatomy of heart veins, and her research shows that blood would be able to flow away through other confluences, through the valve of Vieussens and the thebesian veins.

Edelman and Elzbieta subsequently try it out on corpses' hearts—they inject methylene blue into veins in order to see if it flows away. It does.

But the Professor says, "So what? After all, there was no pressure on those veins."

They inject the blue liquid under pressure and it again finds an outlet.

But the Professor says, "So what? After all, this is just a model. How would a live heart react?"

Well, this is a question nobody can answer because nobody has made such a test on a live heart before. In order to know how a live heart would react, it would be necessary to operate on a live heart.

And on whose live heart is the Professor supposed to operate?

Just a second, we have forgotten about Aga, and Aga has just gone to the library.

Aga Zuchowska goes to the library whenever a new idea comes up. Before she goes there, she says: "Fat chance." For instance, Edelman says: "Who knows, maybe it is possible to operate on bypasses in an acute state." And Aga says, "Fat chance," goes to do some reading, comes back with *The*

American Heart Journal, and triumphantly announces: "Here they say that you are just spewing nonsense." And then a bypass in an acute state is attempted, and everything works out perfectly.

Nowadays, Aga says that when one has pronounced "Fat chance" enough times and then has gone on to see that the man, despite all the experts, turns out to be right, one eventually stops shrugging one's shoulders. Furthermore, one begins to try to forget what all these experts have been writing and instead, upon hearing about some new idea, one quickly tries to adjust to this new way of thinking.

But in those days, Dr. Zuchowska still used to say "Fat chance." So she went to the library and brought back an article from *The Encyclopedia of Thoracic Surgery*. Over thirty years earlier, it turns out, an American surgeon, Claude Beck, used to do something similar but the rate of mortality had proven so high that he'd given up on it. . . .

So, whose live heart? . . .

Now, we have to detour from our subject for a moment to talk about the anterior myocardial infarction with left anterior hemiblock.

This is very important because, up till now, it has never been possible to rescue anybody from this sort of heart attack.

People die in these circumstances in a somewhat peculiar way: they lie quiet, silent, more silent still, yet more quiet, with every passing hour, and gradually everything inside them slowly dies. Legs—liver—kidneys—brain . . . Until one day the heart simply stops and the person is dead. It happens so very quietly, so inadvertently, that a patient on the next bed may not even notice.

When a person with an anterior myocardial infarction with left anterior hemiblock is brought to the hospital, one can be sure that this patient is going to die.

So one day a woman with such a heart attack is brought in. Edelman calls the Professor at his clinic. "This woman is going to die within a few days. The only thing that can save her is a reversal of her blood circulation." Now, this woman doesn't look at all as if she is going to die.

Still, after a few days the woman dies.

Some time later, a man with the same kind of heart attack is brought in. They call the Professor: "If you don't operate on this man . . ."

Within a few days, the man dies. Later, there is another man. Later some young guy, then two women . . .

The Professor comes in every time. He no longer suggests that these people may survive without an operation. He simply looks on in silence, or he asks Edelman: "What do you actually want from me? Do you want me to perform an operation nobody has ever succeeded with before?" To which Edelman answers: "Professor, I am only saying that we won't otherwise have any chance of curing this patient, and nobody but you is capable of performing that operation."

A year passes.

Twelve or thirteen people die.

By the fourteenth case the Professor says: "All right. We'll try."

So let's get back to the Professor's office.

As we recall, he is alone. On the desk in front of him lie Mr. Rzewuski's coronograms, and Mr. Rzewuski is lying in the operating ward.

On the other side of the door, on a chair, Dr. Edelman is sitting and smoking his cigarettes.

The biggest problem at this moment is precisely the fact that Dr. Edelman is sitting in that chair and certainly will not be moving from there.

Why is this such a big problem?

It's simple.

There is only one exit from the office, and it's blocked by Dr. Edelman.

Couldn't the Professor, for instance, say, "Excuse me, just for a moment," and quickly bypass Edelman, and walk away?

Yes, he could. He has even done so once. Before Mr. Rudny. And what? He came back himself, before the day was over, and Mr. Rudny was still waiting for him in the surgery ward, and Edelman with Chetkowska and Zuchowska were still sitting on the chairs of his waiting room.

Anyway, where could he possibly have gone?

Home? They would have found him in no time.

To one of his kids? They would have found him at the latest by the next day.

Out of town? Maybe. . . . But eventually he would always have to come back—and then he would find all of them: Mr. Rzewuski, Edelman, Zuchowska. . . . But perhaps he would not find Mr. Rzewuski anymore.

Mr. Rudny, the one whom he'd come back for before the end of the day, is still alive.

And Mrs. Bubner, the one with blood circulation, is also still alive.

That's right, we have been talking about blood circulation.

"All right, we'll try." This is the point we stopped at before, at that point, and now the Professor is beginning the operation. The other one—on Mrs. Bubner's heart. Let's not mix these two cases. It even makes sense that the Professor is thinking now about this other operation. He is trying to brace himself.

(That time also everybody was saying to him: "But it's crazy, her heart will choke with blood. . . .")

The operating room is silent.

The Professor takes up the main vein, in order to stop the blood leak and see what happens.

(Claude Beck had not taken up the leak, which later caused right heart asthenia and death. So the Professor improves on that method—no, he doesn't allow the use of that word *improve*—he only *alters* Claude Beck's method.)

He is waiting . . .

The heart is working normally. He now joins the main artery to the vein with a special bridge. Arterial blood is beginning to flow into the veins.

He waits again.

The heart moves. Another spasm. Then a few more fast spasms and the heart begins to work slowly, regularly. The blue veins become red from arterial blood and begin to throb. The blood is flowing away—nobody knows exactly where, but it is finding some outlet through some of the smaller runoffs.

Several more minutes pass in silence. The heart is still beating, without any interference.

The Professor mentally finishes off that operation and once again happily realizes that Mrs. Bubner is still alive.

The successful operation on Mr. Rudny had been all over the papers. This story of the reversed blood circulation of Mrs. Bubner he'd reported to a convention of heart surgeons in Bad Nauheim, West Germany, and everybody had risen from their chairs and applauded. Professors Borst and Hoffmeister of West Germany even suggested that this method would now solve the problem of coronary sclerosis, and surgeons in Pittsburgh, for the first time in the United States, started performing this sort of operation based on the Professor's method. However, if the operation on Mr. Rzewuski proved unsuccessful, was anyone going to say, "But at least Mr. Rudny and Mrs. Bubner are still alive"?

No, nobody was going to say that.

Everybody would instead say, "He operated during a heart attack, so he is guilty of Mr. Rzewuski's death."

At this point someone may begin to feel that the Professor has been sitting in his office far too long already, and that it wouldn't hurt to add some dynamics to our story.

Unfortunately, an attempt at escape, which certainly would have animated the whole story, failed. What more was left? Oh, right, God was left.

But not the one with whom the religious Jew, Mr. Bubner, arranged the successful outcome of his wife's operation.

Rather, the God the Professor prays to every Sunday at eleven accompanied by his wife, three children, children-in-law, and a handful of grandchildren.

So the Professor could pray, even in his office. But what for?

Indeed, what for?

That at the last moment, already on the operating table, Rzewuski would change his mind and revoke his consent to the operation? Or maybe that his wife, who is even now crying just outside in the hall, might all of a sudden say no?

Yes, this is what the Professor might now like to pray for.

But—just a second—in refusing to undergo an operation, this man (as the Professor knows very well) would be signing his own death sentence. So is he supposed to be praying for the guy's certain death?

It is true that such operations have not been performed before, or at least, when performed, they were performed differently. But, then, nobody transplanted a heart before Christiaan Barnard either. There always has to be someone who risks, if medicine is going to make any progress at all. (As we can see, the Professor is now including social motivation.) And when is one allowed to risk? When one has deep confidence in the value of such an operation. The Professor has such confidence. He has thoroughly thought through every detail of the proposed intervention, and all his knowledge, his expertise, and his intuition—everything confirms the logic and necessity of what he is planning to do. Besides, there is nothing to be lost here. He knows that without the operation this man is going to die anyway. (Is it certain that Mr. Rzewuski would die without the operation?)

He calls in the general-medicine doctor.

"Are you sure that Mr. Rzewuski would die without this operation?"

"Professor, it is his second heart attack. His second, *extensive* heart attack."

"In that case, he will not survive the operation. . . . Why should we torture him further?"

"Professor, they brought him here all the way from Warsaw not so that he die here, but so that we save him."

This was Dr. Edelman talking now. Oh, it's easy for Dr. Edelman to say such things. If anything happens, nobody will reproach him.

Edelman is absolutely certain that he's right. The Professor is also certain. But it is the Professor, and only the Professor, who will have to confirm it with his own hands.

—Why, I ask Edelman, were you convinced that it was right to operate?

—Because. Because I saw the sense of it and knew that it would work out all right.

—Listen, Marek, I say, perhaps you go for such things so easily because you are so familiar with death . . . ? You were much more familiar with death than, for example, the Professor?

—No, he says. I hope it's not because of that. It's just that when one knows death so well, one has more responsibility for life. Any, even the smallest chance for life becomes extremely important.

(A chance for death was there all the while. The important thing was to make a chance for life.)

33

Careful now. The Professor is about to introduce a new character. Dr. Wroblowna.

"Bring in Doctor Wroblowna," he says.

Everything is clear.

Dr. Wroblowna is an elderly, shy, careful lady, a cardiologist from the Professor's clinic. She would never advise him to do anything improper, to take any kind of untoward risk.

The Professor will ask, "Well, Miss Zofia? What is your advice?" And Miss Zofia will answer, "The best thing is to wait, Professor. After all, we don't know how such a heart will react. . . ." And then the Professor will be able to turn triumphantly to Edelman: "You see, Doctor, my cardiologists won't let me!" (He will stress the word *my*, because Dr. Wroblowna is from his clinic and Dr. Edelman is from the city hospital. Or maybe that's just my mistaken impression, and the word *my* simply implies that the Professor, the head of the clinic, has to take into account the opinions of his doctors.)

So Dr. Wroblowna comes in. Shy, she blushes, looks down. Then she says in a very low voice:

"It is necessary to operate, Professor."

No! That beats all!

"Wroblowna," the Professor cries, "even you're against me, too?"

He pretends that he is joking, but he begins to have an odd feeling, a feeling that will not leave him till the end of the day.

When he gets up from behind his desk—gathering up the coronograms and heading toward the operating room where Mr. Rzewuski, asleep, already awaits him, along with the surgeons in their blue masks and the nurses—he will be unable to shake the feeling that he is absolutely alone, despite the presence of all these people.

Alone with the heart, which is moving in its sack like a tiny, frightened animal.

For it is still moving.

Everything I've written so far I've shown to various people—and they don't understand a thing. Why haven't I talked about how he managed to survive? It isn't even clear how he managed to survive, and already we have him sitting behind the door of the Professor's office. And, after all, he *has* to be sitting there; otherwise, if he weren't, the Professor would have gotten home a long time ago, he'd be in the middle of watching the TV news, all relaxed and quiet.

Therefore he has to be behind that door, along with Aga and Elzbieta Chetkowska. Although there is no Elzbieta anymore. I mean—she is there while they are sitting there waiting, but she no longer exists as I write about that waiting. All that's left of her is the Dr. Elzbieta Chetkowska Prize awarded for outstanding achievements in the field of cardiology.

They founded that prize based on royalties from their book *Infarction*. During that research on starvation Edelman hadn't been able to participate because at the Ghetto hospital he'd only been a messenger, but now, with this one, he'd been able to describe everything he knew about people with heart diseases. Tosia Goliborska told me that in the Ghetto hospital they had had an inkling of his other activities—and that they should not ask him questions about them—so that therefore they did not demand much from him, only that each day he deliver the blood from the typhoid victims to the epidemiology station. The rest of the day he could spend at his place in the Umschlagplatz, standing there every day for six weeks until four hundred thousand people had passed by him on their way into the train cars.

The movie *Requiem for 500,000* shows them filing in. One can even see the bread loaves in their hands. A German cameraman stood at the train car's entrance and photographed the surging crowd, the stumbling old women, the mothers dragging their children by the hands. They are running with this bread toward us and toward the Swedish journalists who have come here to Warsaw to gather material about the Ghetto; they are running toward Inger, a Swedish journalist who is looking at the screen with dumbfounded blue eyes, trying to comprehend why so many people are running toward the train car—and then, suddenly, the shots are heard. What a relief it is when they start shooting! What a relief it is when puffs of dust veil the running crowd and their loaves of bread and the narrator informs us about the outbreak of the uprising, so that it now becomes possible to explain it all to Inger in a matter-of-fact way (*The uprising's broken out, this is April forty-three*). . . .

I tell Marek about this scene and I say how it's really a well-thought-out sequence. It's great how the explosions veil the people—and at that point he begins to scream. He screams that I probably consider the people who were surging into the train cars to have been worse than the ones who were shooting. Of course, I do, absolutely, everybody does, even that American, the professor who recently visited Marek and told him, "You were going like sheep to your deaths." That American professor landed once on some French beach, scrambled for four or five hundred meters under withering fire without swerving or even crouching down, got wounded, and now he believes that if one has run across such a beach, he later has the right to say "Men should run," or "Men should shoot," or "You were going like sheep." The professor's wife added that those shots were needed by future generations: the death of people dying in silence means nothing because it leaves nothing behind, whereas those who shoot leave a legend behind—for her and her American children.

He'd very well understood why the professor—who still had the scars from his wounds, had medals and academic tenure—why he wanted to include those shots in his history. But he nevertheless tried to explain to him several things—how to die in a gas chamber is by no means worse than to die in battle, and that the only undignified death is when one attempts to survive at the expense of somebody else. But he'd been unable to explain anything, and instead he'd started yelling all over again. Some woman who was in the room tried to offer apologies on his behalf: "Excuse him, please," she'd pleaded in embarrassment. "One has to excuse him . . ."

—My dear, Edelman says, you have to understand this once and for all. Those people went quietly and with dignity. It is a horrendous thing, when one is going so quietly to one's death. It is infinitely more difficult than to go out shooting. After all, it is much easier to die firing—for us it was much easier to die than it was for someone who first boarded a train car, then rode the train, then dug a hole, then undressed naked. . . . Do you understand now? he asks.

—Yes, I say. I see. Because it is indeed easier, even for us, to look at their death when they are shooting than when they are digging a hole for themselves. . . .

I once saw a crowd on Zelazna Street. People on the street were swarming around this barrel—a simple wooden barrel with a Jew on top of it. He was old and short, and he had a long beard.

Next to him there were two German officers. (Two beautiful, tall men next to this small, bowed Jew.) And those Germans, tuft by tuft, were chopping off this Jew's long beard with huge tailor's shears, splitting their sides with laughter all the while.

The surrounding crowd was also laughing. Because, objectively, it really was funny: a little man on a wooden barrel with his beard growing shorter by the moment as it disappeared under the tailor's shears. Just like a movie gag.

At that time the Ghetto did not exist yet, and one might not have sensed the grim premonition in that scene. After all, nothing really horrible was happening to that Jew: only that it was now possible to put him on a barrel with impunity, that people were beginning to realize that such activity wouldn't be punished and that it provoked laughter.

But you know what?

At that moment I realized that the most important thing on earth was going to be never letting myself be pushed onto the top of that barrel. Never, by anybody. Do you understand?

Everything I was to do later, I was doing in order not to let myself get pushed up there.

—It was the beginning of the war and you could still have left the country. Your friends were still fleeing to places without barrels . . .

—Those were different kinds of people. They were wonderful boys from civilized families. They had excellent grades at school, telephones in their houses, and beautiful paintings on their walls. Originals, not some reproductions. I was nothing compared to them. I wasn't any member of the high life. I had poorer grades, I couldn't sing as well, I couldn't ride a bicycle, and I didn't even have a house because my mother died when I was fourteen. (*Colitis ulceroza*. It's odd: later, the first patient I had in my life suffered from the same thing. Only, by that time there existed prednisone and penicillin, so we cured him in a couple of weeks.)

What were we talking about?

—That some friends did leave.

—You see, Hanna, before the war I was telling my fellow Jews that their place was here, in Poland. That we would build socialism here, and that they should stay here. So when they stayed, and the war then began, and everything that was to happen in this war to the Jews was beginning to happen—how was I supposed to leave?

After the war, some of those friends turned out to be managers of Japanese corporations, or physicists in American nuclear agencies, or professors at colleges. As I told you, they were talented people.

—But by that time you had already pulled yourself up to their level. You had hero status. They could accept you in their glorious class.

—They would ask me to come. But I had seen four hundred thousand people off at the Umschlagplatz. I myself, me, in person. They'd all passed by me while I stood there at the gate . . .

Listen, Hanna, do me a favor, stop asking me those nonsense questions. "Why did you stay?" "Why did you stay?"

—But I am not asking you about it at all.

— . . .

—Well?

—Well what?

—Tell me about the flowers. Or whatever. It doesn't matter what. But it can be about the flowers. How you get them every year on the anniversary of the uprising, without knowing who they are from. Thirty-two bunches so far.

—Thirty-one. In 1968, I didn't get any flowers.* I felt bad about that, but already the next year I was getting them again, and I am still getting them up to this day. Once they were marsh marigolds, last year they were roses—always yellow flowers of some sort. They are delivered by a florist without so much as a word.

—I am not sure, Marek, whether we should write about this. I mean, anonymous yellow flowers? It smacks of cheap literature. I must say that kitschy stories somehow seem to stick to you. Those prostitutes, for instance, who would give you a bagel every day. By the way, do you think it would be proper to write that there were prostitutes in the Ghetto?

—I don't know. Probably it wouldn't be. In the Ghetto there should only have been martyrs and Joans of Arc, right? But if you want to know, in the bunker on Mila Street, together with Anielewicz's group, there were some prostitutes and even a pimp. A big, tattooed guy, with huge biceps, who was their boss. They were good, clever, resourceful girls. Our group got to that bunker after our area began to burn. They were all there—Anielewicz, Celina, Lutek, Jurek Wilner—and we were so happy that we were together again. These girls gave us some food, and Guta had Juno cigarettes. That was one of the best days in the Ghetto.

When we came back later on and everything had already happened to them—there wasn't any Anielewicz anymore, nor Lutek, nor Jurek Wilner—we found those girls in the basement next door.

The next day we headed down into the sewers.

Everybody got in, I was the last one, and one of the girls

*During 1968, a power struggle in the Polish Communist Party included an astonishingly virulent anti-Semitic campaign. Thousands of Jewish professionals were sacked from their jobs and many left the country.

40

asked whether she could join us in escaping to the Aryan side. And I said no.

So you see.

I only ask you one thing: don't make me explain today why I said no then.

—Earlier did you ever have a chance of getting from the Ghetto to the Aryan side?

—Actually, I used to go to the Aryan side, legally, every day. As the hospital messenger, every day I carried blood samples from the typhoid victims for tests at a lab over on Nowogrodzka Street.

I had a pass. There were just a few passes in the Ghetto at that time: at the hospital in Czyste, at the community council, and at our hospital, where I was the only one who had one. Those people from the council, they were dignitaries, they would go to offices and travel in carriages. But I would just walk, wearing my armband on the street, among people, and all those people would gaze at me and at that armband. With curiosity, with sympathy, sometimes with a sneer . . .

I would walk like that every day around 8 A.M. for a couple of years, and in the end nothing bad ever happened to me. Nobody ever stopped me, nobody called a policeman, no one even laughed. People only looked at me. Only looked at me. . . .

—What I meant, Marek, is why didn't you simply stay on the Aryan side?

—I don't know. Today one no longer knows things like why.

—You were a nobody before the war. So, how did it happen that three years later you became a member of the command group of the Jewish Combat Organization? You were one of five people chosen from among the three hundred thousand people who were still there.

—I wasn't the one who was supposed to be there. It should

have been . . . Well, it doesn't matter. Let's call him "Adam."
He graduated before the war from military college and took
part in the September 1939 campaign and in the defense of
Modlin. He was famous for his courage. For many years he
was a real idol of mine.

One day the two of us were walking together along Leszno
Street, there were crowds of people, and all of a sudden some
SS men started shooting.

The crowd scrambled away desperately. And so did he.

You know, I had never before suspected that he could be
afraid of anything. And there he was, my idol, running
away.

Because he was used to always having a weapon by his
side: in the military college, later in the defense of Warsaw
in September, and in Modlin. The others had weapons, but
he had a weapon, too, so therefore he could be brave. But
when it happened that the others were firing their arms and
he couldn't shoot, he became another man.

It all actually happened without a single word, from one
day to the next: he simply quit all activity. And when the
first meeting of the command group was about to be held,
he was useless for participating in it. So I went instead.

He had a girlfriend, Ania. One day, they took her to Pawiak
Prison—she managed to get out later on—but the day they
took her, he broke down completely. He came to see us,
leaned his hands on the table, and started telling us that we
were all lost, that they would slaughter us all, and that since
we were young we should escape to the forest and join the
partisans instead of attempting to form an underground here
in the city.

Nobody interrupted him.

After he'd left, somebody said: "It's because they have
taken her away. He has no reason to live anymore. Now he
will get killed." Everybody had to have somebody to act for,

somebody to be the center of his life. Activity was the only chance for survival. One had to do something, to have somewhere to go.

All this bustle might not have had any importance, because everybody was getting killed anyway, but at least one wasn't just waiting his turn idly.

I was busy at the Umschlagplatz. With the aid of our people in the Ghetto police, I was supposed to select out those whom we needed the most at the time. One day I pulled out a guy and a young woman—he had worked in the printing shop, and she had been an excellent liaison officer. They both died soon afterward—he in the uprising, and she by way of a later trip to the Umschlagplatz—but before that he managed to print an underground paper and she managed to distribute this paper.

I know. You want to ask, what sense did it have?

No sense at all. Thanks to that, one wasn't standing on a barrel. That's all.

There was an emergency room at the Umschlagplatz. Students from the nurses' college worked there—this was, by the way, the only school in the Ghetto. Luba Blum was the headmistress and she made sure that everything there was run like in a real, first-rate school: snow-white robes, starched caps, perfect discipline. In order to pull somebody out from the lines at the Umschlagplatz, it was necessary to prove to the Germans that the person was seriously ill. They would send those sick people home in ambulances: till the last moment, the Germans tried to maintain the illusion in people that they were leaving in those trains to work, and only a healthy person could work, right? So these girls from the emergency room, those nurses, would break the legs of those people who had to be saved. They would wedge a leg up against a wooden block and then smash it with another block. All this in their shiny white robes of model students.

People who were waiting to be loaded onto the trains were herded together in a school building. They would take them out floor by floor, so that from the first floor the people would tend to flee up to the second floor, and from the second to the third, but there were only four floors and on the fourth floor their activity and energy would simply give out, because it was impossible to go any higher. There was a big gym on this fourth floor, and several hundred people would be lying there on the floor. Nobody would stand or walk, nobody would even move. People would just be lying there, apathetic and silent.

There was a niche in this gym. And in this niche one day several Ukrainian guards—six, maybe eight—were raping a young girl. They waited in line and then raped her. After the line was finished, this girl left the niche and she walked across the whole gym, stumbling against the reclining people. She was very pale, naked, and bleeding, and she slouched down into a corner. The crowd saw everything, and nobody said a word. Nobody so much as moved, and the silence continued.

—Did you see that yourself, or somebody told you?

—I saw it. I was standing at the end of the gym and saw everything.

—You were standing in that gym?

—Yes. One day I told Elzbieta about this incident. She asked me, "And you? What did you do then?" "I didn't do anything," I told her. "Anyway, I can see that it's no use talking to you about it. You don't understand a thing!"

—I don't understand why you got so mad. Elzbieta's response was the reaction of any normal person.

—I know. I also know what a normal person is supposed to do in such circumstances. When a woman is being raped, every normal person rushes to her rescue, right?

—If you'd rushed by yourself, they would have killed you.

But if you had all gotten up from the floor, all of you could have easily overpowered those Ukrainians.

—Well, nobody got up. Nobody was any longer capable of getting up from that floor. Those people were capable of only one thing: waiting for the trains. But, why are we talking about it?

—I don't know. You were saying before how it was necessary to keep busy.

—I was busy at the Umschlagplatz. . . . And that girl is still alive, you know?

My word of honor. She is married, has two kids, and is very happy.

—You were busy at the Umschlagplatz . . .

—And one day I selected out Pola Lifszyc. The next day she went to her house and she saw that her mother wasn't there—her mother was already in a column marching toward the Umschlagplatz. Pola ran after this column alone, she ran after this column from Leszno Street to Stawki—her fiancé gave her a lift in his riksa so that she could catch up—and she made it. At the last minute she managed to merge into the crowd so as to be able to get on the train with her mother.

Everybody knows about Korczak, right?* Korczak was a hero because he went to death with his children of his own free will.

But Pola Lifszyc, who went with her mother—who knows about Pola Lifszyc?

And Pola could have easily crossed to the Aryan side because she was young, pretty, she didn't look Jewish, and she'd have had a hundred times better chance.

*Janusz Korczak (né Henryk Goldszmit) was a famous writer of children's books and director of a Warsaw orphanage who, though exempted from deportation, chose to accompany his young wards to Treblinka.

—Marek, you once mentioned the life tickets. Who distributed them?

—There were forty thousand tickets—little white chits of paper with a stamp. The Germans gave them to the community council and said: "Distribute them among yourselves. Those who have the tickets will stay in the Ghetto. All the others must go to the Umschlagplatz."

It was two days before the conclusion of the liquidation action, in September. The head doctor of our hospital, Mrs. Heller, got some fifteen tickets, and said: "I'm not going to pass these out."

Any of the doctors could have distributed these tickets but everybody thought that she would give them to those who deserved them most.

Listen to me: "Who deserved them most." Is there any standard that can be used to decide who has the right to live? There is no such standard. But delegations of people went to Mrs. Heller begging her to distribute the tickets, so finally she agreed to.

She gave Frania a ticket. And Frania had a mother and a sister. All those who had tickets were being gathered together near Zamenhofa Street, and all about them a crowd of people who didn't have tickets was scrambling. Among those people, Frania's mother was standing. She didn't want to leave Frania, even though Frania had already joined the ranks of the reprieved. Frania kept saying: "Mother, go already." She was pushing her away with her hand. "Mother, go away."

Yes, Frania did survive.

She later saved the lives of a dozen or so people. She carried one guy out of the Warsaw uprising. In general, she behaved extraordinarily.

One such ticket went to Mrs. Tenenbaum, the head nurse. She was a friend of Berenson, the famous attorney, the defense lawyer in the Brzesc trial. She had a daughter who hadn't gotten a ticket. So Mrs. Tenenbaum gave her ticket to her daughter and said, "Hold this for a second, I'll be right back," and she went upstairs and swallowed a flaskful of Luminal.

We found her the next day, she was still alive.

Do you think we should have tried to save her?

—What happened to the daughter who now had the ticket?

—First, answer: Should we have tried to save her?

—You know, Tosia Goliborska told me that her mother also swallowed poison. "And that moron, my brother-in-law," she told me, "he saved her. Can you imagine such a moron? To save her just so that a few days later she could be dragged to the Umschlagplatz. . . ."

—When the liquidation action started and they were gathering up people from the first floor of our hospital, one woman upstairs was in labor. A doctor and a nurse were with her. And when the baby was born, the doctor handed it to the nurse, and the nurse laid it on one pillow, and smothered it with another one. The baby whimpered for a while and then grew silent.

This woman was nineteen years old. The doctor didn't say a thing to her. Not a word. And this woman knew herself what she was supposed to do.

I'm glad that you haven't asked me today, "And did this woman survive?" the way you asked about the doctor who gave cyanide to the children.

Yes, she did survive. She is a very famous pediatrician.

—So what happened to Mrs. Tenenbaum's daughter?

—Nothing; she also died. But before that she had a few really good months: she was in love with a guy, and in his presence she was always serene, smiling. She had some really good months.

That French guy from *L'Express* asked me whether people in the Ghetto fell in love. Well . . .

—Excuse me. Did you also get a ticket?

—Yes. I was standing in the fifteenth row of five, in the same column in which Frania and Mrs. Tenenbaum's daughter were already standing, and I noticed a friend of mine and her brother. So I quickly pulled them into the column. Only, other people had been doing the same thing, so that in our crowd there were already not forty thousand but forty-four thousand people.

Therefore the Germans simply counted out the people and sent the last four thousand to the Umschlagplatz. Somehow I managed to squeeze in with the first forty thousand.

—So this French guy was asking you . . .

—. . . whether people fell in love. Well, to be with someone was the only way to survive in the Ghetto. One would secret oneself somewhere with the other person—in a bed, in a basement, anywhere—and until the next action one was not alone anymore.

One person had had his mother taken away, somebody else's father had been shot and killed, or a sister taken away in a shipment. So if someone, somehow, by some miracle escaped and was still alive, he had to stick to some other living human being.

People were drawn to one another as never before, as never in normal life. During the last liquidation action they would run to the Jewish Council in search of a rabbi or anybody who could marry them, and then they would go to the Umschlagplatz as a married couple.

Tosia's niece went with her boyfriend to Pawia Street—at 1 Pawia Street lived some rabbi who married them—and immediately after that wedding, some Ukrainians arrived and wanted to take her away. One of them put the barrel of his rifle up against her belly. So he, her husband, pushed that barrel away, covering her belly with his hand. She, by the way, ended up going to the Umschlagplatz anyway, and he, with a blown hand, managed to run away to the Aryan side and later died in the 1944 Warsaw uprising.

But this was precisely what mattered: that there be someone ready to cover your belly with his hand should that prove necessary.

—When the whole operation started, the Umschlagplatz and all that, did you—you and your friends—immediately understand what it meant?

—Oh, yes. On July 22, 1942, an ordinance about "relocation of the population to the East" was posted all over the Ghetto, and that very night we were pasting pieces of paper over the ordinance: "Relocation means Death."

The next day, prisoners from jail and old people were taken to the Umschlagplatz. It took the whole day because there were six thousand prisoners to be transported. People were standing along sidewalks, looking—and you know, it was completely silent. It all happened in such an eerie silence . . .

Later, there were no more prisoners and no more old people, and no more beggars, and it was still necessary to deliver ten thousand people a day to the Umschlagplatz. The Jewish police were supposed to accomplish this under German supervision. The Germans would say: things will be quiet and nobody will be shot so long as every day, by 4 P.M., you deliver ten thousand people to the trains. (Because at four the transport was scheduled to leave.) So people were told: "We have to deliver ten thousand, the rest will survive." And the Jewish police would gather up the people themselves: first in the street, then they would circle a house, pull people from apartments . . .

We later executed some of those policemen. The police commander, Szerynski, Lejkin, a few more.

The second day of the action, on July 23rd, representatives of all the political parties gathered and for the first time they discussed armed resistance. Everybody was already determined and the question was only how to get arms, but after a few hours someone came in and announced that the action had been interrupted and that there would be no more relocations. Not everyone believed this, but the news immediately calmed the atmosphere down and no decisions were made.

And actually, the majority of people still didn't believe that it meant death. "Is it conceivable that they would kill a *whole* nation?" they would ask themselves, and this would reassure them. It is necessary to deliver those ten thousand to the square, in order to save the rest . . .

In the evening of the first day of the action, Czerniakow, the community council chairman, committed suicide. It was the only rainy day. Except for this one day, during the entire action, it was sunny every day. The day Czerniakow died, the setting sun was red and we were sure that it would rain the next day, but it turned out sunny.

—What did you need rain for?

—For nothing. I am just telling you how it was.

As far as Czerniakow goes, we were resentful. We thought that he shouldn't have . . .

—I know, we have spoken about that already.

—Oh, yes?

You know, Hanna, after the war was over someone told me that Lejkin, this policeman we killed in the Ghetto, at that time, after seventeen years of marriage, had had his first child, and he'd thought that he might save that child's life with that cleverness of his.

—Do you want to tell me anything more about the action?

—No. The action was over.
I was alive.

It so happened that all of them—Mr. Rudny, Mrs. Bubner, and Mr. Wilczkowski, the well-known Alpinist—had their heart attacks on Friday during the day or at night, and Saturday was for each of them a day when they suddenly had no more errands to run. Saturday found each of them lying immobile, under a Xylocaine drip, thinking.

Engineer Wilczkowski, for example, was thinking about the mountains, more precisely, about a specific mountain peak goldened by sunshine (this is how he expressed it, poetically), atop which he was sitting and unfurling rope—not any of the mountaintops in the Alps or in Ethiopia, not even one in the Himalayas, but rather a peak in the Polish Tatra mountains, Mieguszowiecki, or perhaps Zabi Mnich, where one September he had accomplished a very pretty climb up the west face. Mr. Rudny (first vein transplant in acute state) for his part was envisioning machinery, all modern, of course, imported, British or Swiss, and all of it in working order because no parts were missing. Mrs. Bubner, on the other hand (reversed blood circulation), had before her eyes an injection molding machine. Her employee was using it to manufacture plastic parts, but later it was she herself who would put them into boiling paint because this was the most responsible part of the work. Later still, she would assemble the whole ballpoint pen (obviously, she had a certificate from Customs for the Swiss end pieces she had managed to get through private channels), slap on a label, and put the whole pen into a box.

This was what Dr. Edelman's patients were thinking about, lying under the Xylocaine drip.

Under the drip, one usually ends up thinking about the most important things.

For the head doctor, Mrs. Heller, the most important thing had been who deserved the life ticket. And for Mr. Rudny, the most important thing was the spare parts for the machines. If Mrs. Heller gave the ticket to Mr. Rudny, it would have been a ticket for machines, because they are Mr. Rudny's life, as Mrs. Bubner's life is ballpoint pens, and Mr. Wilczkowski's mountain peaks.

As far as Mr. Rzewuski is concerned, he wasn't thinking at all.

If Mr. Rzewuski, like Mrs. Bubner or Mr. Rudny, had been thinking about the best thing in his life, he would doubtlessly have been thinking of a factory that was turned over to him when he was twenty-eight years old and taken away from him when he was forty-three. He would have been sensing a metallic smell and hearing someone coming in with a blueprint and he would know that something was just being created, something was going to be possible to look at, possible to check on, to measure, and he would be feeling impatient, watching as the metal was being shaped, because he so much wanted already to be able to touch the prototype he had seen moments earlier in the drawing. . . .

("The factory," Mr. Rzewuski once said, "was for me the same as the Ghetto was for Doctor Edelman: the most important thing that happened in my life. Activity. A chance to test oneself. *A truly macho adventure.*")

Mr. Rzewuski would have certainly been thinking about all that as he lay under the i.v. drip, if he thought about anything at all. But, as I have said, he was not thinking about anything while the Professor was still sitting in his office, sunk in thought, and the anesthesiologist was already busying himself around his body, nor a few hours later, when the Professor and Edelman and Dr. Chetkowska looked on gladly as the blinking light traversed the screen of the monitor. All that time he'd been experiencing only one sensation—pain—and nothing could have been more important than easing that pain, if only for a moment.

It was the first attempt through the middle of western approaches and probably it was not September after all; in any case, it was very sunny there during the climb. Later, looking down from above, they saw the Morskie Oko lake, and in the background, the jagged world and the Babia Gora mountain. The Englishman Mallory, when asked why he was trying to climb Mount Everest, replied: *because it is there*. Because it is there. That golden peak remained far away throughout the day all Saturday (prednisone was added to the Xylocaine), he was scaling it, he could see it very clearly but was unable to approach it even by a single millimeter, and he suddenly realized that he would never make it to that sunny place.

He started thinking about his chances. He hadn't had an accident so far in the mountains, but this did not calm him down, because someone could always cross the line of his destiny. After all, there are hobgoblins who bring bad luck to mountain people. Before his group's expedition to Ethiopia, their hobgoblin (it only turned out later that he was a hobgoblin) had been assigned luggage container number eight, which he did not want to carry; somebody else took it. There were eight men, they departed on the eighth, and the man who took container number eight slipped off the moving truck's canvas, something no one was ever able to understand since they had all been sleeping on that canvas tied down with ropes. On Deyrenfurth's expedition to Mount Everest a Hindu died of exhaustion and the hobgoblin was the last person who saw him, and that Hindu, by the way, had been wearing the hobgoblin's parka. The whole night from Saturday to Sunday, Wilczkowski was thinking about his own place, and even though he was doing his best to think absolutely objectively, he arrived at a conclusion that his coordinate did not cross anything suspicious, which reassured him a lot.

The four reels in the British machine should be adjusted in such a way that they all are synchronized, so that there isn't any stress and the material doesn't snap. One adjusts them through a sort of box that includes a lock ring around a conical disk, and when the material on the reels—be it ribbon, or elastic, or some other sort of strap—has achieved the requisite humidity and speed, and all the reels are perfectly synchronized one to the next, *that* is a wonderful moment, because one knows one has achieved total mastery over the entire machine.

The machines were then oiled, the cylinders he'd managed to adjust perfectly were swinging rhythmically, and Mr. Rudny could spend a few moments daydreaming about his little lot, how it was going to be necessary to dig it up, and how actually it might not be bad to build some sort of bower there.

His wife said that who knows, maybe they should build a little house there, you know, a summer cabin—everybody is having such cabins built nowadays.

His wife used to tell him that, so far, anyway, they had always managed to achieve everything they'd most wanted in their lives: he had filled their apartment with that highly fashionable, light-colored furniture—only the cabinet's doors were lacquered black—they had gotten the coupon for a washing machine without having to wait at all, they were managing a family vacation every year, and it had never ever happened that they'd sold out the boneless veal before they reached her turn at the store. So certainly, if they only busied themselves a bit, they were going to be able to have this cabin—his wife used to talk like that. Until she saw him that day from a distance through the half-open door of the intensive care unit, she'd imagined that they'd managed to put together everything that really matters in a person's life.

Ballpoint pens could be sold only through bookstores. Newsstands and stationery shops were not allowed to take merchandise from small private factories like hers, so she was totally dependent on the bookstores. A bookstore's manager could take a thousand or two at a pop, and Mrs. Bubner had to do everything to avoid having her merchandise remain unsold.

She had her heart attack just after she came home from the trial (she received a one-year sentence, suspended to three years' probation). During the trial it turned out that the rate had been standardized: all the makers of ballpoint pens bribed the bookstore managers exactly 6 percent, that is, between ten and twenty thousand zlotys for each consignment.

In the court it also turned out that it wasn't just the ones who gave the bribes who had heart problems. Those who served as intermediaries were in even worse shape: one of the intermediaries had to take nitroglycerin every once in a while, and the woman judge would order a short recess each time: "Just a second," she would say. "Let's wait for the nitroglycerin to dissolve; and please, don't be so anxious."

In the worst shape of all, however, were those who *accepted* the bribes: the bookstore managers themselves. One had already had a heart attack, and the court doctor authorized him to testify for only one hour, so that the woman judge had to look at her watch all the while, and after exactly one hour she would order a recess. In fairness, it should be stressed that this judge had a really good and understanding attitude toward all those suffering from heart disorders: manufacturers, intermediaries, and bookstore managers.

As far as she, Mrs. Bubner, was concerned, during the trial she had not yet required medical care. She had her heart attack only after the trial, at her home, and she'd even managed to rise from her stretcher and ask her neighbor to put her dachshund to sleep with the best shot available.

"Doctor Edelman approached me later and said, 'You have to have the operation, Mrs. Bubner.' So I started crying, and at first I said, 'No.' He said, 'Believe me, Mrs. Bubner, you really should agree to it.' "

(Because Mrs. Bubner's case was precisely an anterior myocardial infarction with left anterior hemiblock—the kind with which people grow more and more silent and quiescent because everything inside them is slowly, gradually dying. And Mrs. Bubner was the fourteenth person, when the Professor no longer asked, "What actually do you want from me?" and only said, "All right, we'll try." And so Dr. Edelman was saying, "You really should agree, Mrs. Bubner, believe me. . . .")

". . . and it occurred to me at that moment how my late husband had been such a good, religious man. He used to say, 'Well, Mania, but God *does* exist.' He was very active in the Jewish community. After meetings in the Guild he would never go to Malinowa Restaurant with the others; instead he'd come directly home. And if I sometimes wanted to have a drink with some of the other people, he would say, 'All right, Mania, only give me your purse, so that you don't lose it.' So if a man like this requests something of his God, surely this God would not refuse him. Even while I was in Mostowski Jail for a month, before the trial, I remained calm, for I knew that the door would eventually open up because it was impossible that my late husband wouldn't arrange it for me. And guess what, Mrs. Krall? He did, didn't he? A bookkeeper from the Guild came and paid my bail and I was allowed conditional freedom until the trial.

"So that time I also ended up saying, 'Don't worry, Doctor, you'll see, he is going to arrange everything just right.' "

(Soon after she'd spoken those words, the Professor was taking up the main vein in Mrs. Bubner's heart in order to block the blood flow and redirect the arterial blood into the veins, and as it turned out, to everyone's happiness, that blood somehow was finding its confluence. . . .)

Before they brought in the new, imported machines, they had sent Mr. Rudny to England, to Newcastle, for training. Mr. Rudny noticed there that far fewer mistakes had to be ferreted out by the English quality-control people than by the ones in his factory and that in England it simply never happened that a machine had to be stopped for lack of a spare part.

When he returned to Lodz he would dream of attaining the same efficiency as the machines in Newcastle. Unfortunately, one could fret oneself to one's very limits and still not be able to find the various required parts, there was still all sorts of waste, and on top of everything, he couldn't find a common language with the young workers.

The head of the factory says that in the old days the loyalty toward one's boss was different because it was difficult to find jobs. Today, workers' kids go to college; this is all to the good, it's only that later there are no people left to work in the factories and whenever a new person does come to work, especially those with vocational training, he immediately becomes all fresh and everything because he well understands his position.

So when Mr. Rudny came back from the hospital after the operation (it was that intervention in acute state when for a while the question had been who was going to get there first: the heart attack or the doctors, the doctors or God—it was that intervention before which the Professor had tried to leave the clinic and not come back; but he had come back, that very day, late in the afternoon; and, as a matter of fact, the Professor was not the only one who'd left. Edelman had also left, even though he had insisted so strongly that they perform that operation; he'd said: "I'm going to go and think," because he also knew of books where it was said that such interventions should not be performed; he'd come back after a couple of hours, and then it had been Elzbieta Chetkowska who was yelling, "Where did you go? Don't you know that every minute counts?!")—when Mr. Rudny came back to the factory after that operation that had been covered all over in the press, he was immediately transferred to a quieter department. In particular, they had looked for a place without imported machines with their impossible-to-find spare parts and young, highly trained workers, so they'd moved him over to the oil department. "Mr. Rudny's health, and nothing but his health, was the reason for this transfer," the manager points out, "and not, as Mr. Rudny falsely believes, the fact that he'd gone to the safety-control board and told them that Mr. Nowak, who had been on sick leave for ten days, wasn't just sick, but that he had had a work-related accident. It is very embarrassing for the factory when a work-related accident only gets reported after a ten-day delay like that, but, as I have said, that wasn't the case here and this was not the reason we gave Mr. Rudny the quieter job."

At his new workplace, Mr. Rudny was checking up on the greases. What kind of work was that! Look at a machine, write a report, that's all. Mr. Rudny understood very well that it was important, responsible work, because as long as a high-speed machine is well oiled it will work for many years, but there were no immediate rewards with such work.

The manager does not understand what I am getting at with all my interest in Mr. Rudny's health.

Perhaps I think that the factory was responsible for Mr. Rudny's illness? I don't think so at all. The manager adds that after each trip to a cooperating factory, where he has to beg for spare parts and a higher quality of thread, his own stomach ulcer acts up all over again. And the chief mechanic, Mr. Rudny's immediate boss (spare parts not for a few machines but for the whole factory!), has already twice been taken to a hospital on the very verge of a heart attack, and if I want, he'll measure his own blood pressure right then and there, it's the end of the trimester and he's certain it won't be less than 180/110.

All three of them, Mrs. Bubner, the engineer Wilczkowski, and Mr. Rudny, had all kinds of time to think those Saturdays. And what each of them was thinking was how they sure didn't want another heart attack.

One can resolve not to have another heart attack; in the same way, by choosing a certain life-style, one can accept the good possibility of a heart attack.

Therefore, upon returning home, Mrs. Bubner closed down her shop. It is obligatory to save all the documentation for five years and she still has her ballpoint pens, one from each model. From time to time, she takes them out, cleans them, and examines them—shiny, four colors each, with labels and invoice included. And then she puts them back into the box, stores them away, and slowly goes out for a walk.

Mr. Rudny, on the other hand, who recently has been transferred back to his old department because some imported machines have again arrived (this time from Switzerland), says to himself: "Calmly. Calmly. Even if there is a part missing, I do not have to try to revive an old one or to twist my neck in order to make a new one myself. If there is a part missing, all I'm supposed to do is to file a formal order, and everything'll be okay."

And indeed: he files a written order, and everything is okay.

And if sometimes he breaks his word to himself, it really is just for a moment. And if he feels pain coming on in his breastbone area, he goes to a doctor, hears the advice—"Mr. Rudny, you should enjoy your life and not worry so much about machines"—and returns to filing his orders once again.

He doesn't feel pain anymore and he comes to the hospital only for social reasons, as a guest. On June 5th, the anniversary of his operation, he brings three bunches of flowers. He hands one to the Professor, the other one to Dr. Edelman, and he takes the third one to Dr. Chetkowska and puts it on her grave in the Radogoszcz Cemetery.

The action was over and you were alive . . .

—There were sixty thousand Jews left in the Ghetto. Those who'd managed to survive now understood everything: just what "relocation" meant and that it was impossible to wait any longer. We decided to create one military organization for the whole Ghetto, which was not simple because we didn't have confidence in each other, we in the Zionists or they in us, but at that point, of course, it didn't matter anymore. We created one organization: the Jewish Combat Organization.

There were five hundred of us. In January there was another action and there were only eighty people left. During that January action, for the first time, some people were refusing to go to their deaths voluntarily. We shot and killed a few Germans on Muranowska, Franciszkanska, Mila, and Zamenhofa streets. Those were the first shots in the Ghetto, and they made a big impression on the Aryan side: this was before the big armed operations of the Polish resistance movement. Wladyslaw Szlengel, a poet who continued to compose poetry in the Ghetto in which he expressed his revulsion at the prospect of submissive acquiescence in one's own death, managed to write a poem about those shots. It was called "Counterattack":

. . . Do you hear, oh German God,
the Jews praying in their wild houses,
grasping crowbars and wrenched-out stakes in their hands?
We beseech you, God, for bloody struggle,
we beg you for a sudden death.
Let our eyes before their dimming
not be forced to gaze upon slowly moving rails,
but Lord, give our hands precision. . . .
Like the scarlet, blood-red flowers
on Niska and Mila streets, in Muranow
the fire blossoms from our barrels.
This is our spring, this, our counterattack,
this, the wine of battle gone to our heads,
this is our partisan forest—
the back alleys of Dzika and Ostrowska. . . .

For the sake of exactitude I'll tell you that those "our barrels" from which the fire blossomed—at that time there were ten of them in the Ghetto. We'd gotten those guns from the Popular Army.*

Anielewicz's group, which was taken to the Umschlagplatz and did not have arms, started hitting the Germans with bare fists. The group of Pelc, the eighteen-year-old printer, when taken to the square, refused to board the train, and van

*Popular Army (AL), one of the independent clandestine armed organizations operating in Poland during the war; this one was affiliated with the Moscow-oriented Communist party.

Oeppen, the commander of the Treblinka camp, shot all of them, sixty men, on the spot. I remember, the Kosciuszko radio station then started broadcasting appeals encouraging people to struggle. Some woman kept shouting "To arms, to arms" with a sound-effects background imitating the jangle of weapons. We were wondering what they were using to make that sound, because as far as we were concerned, we had sixty guns at that point, from the Polish Workers' Party and from the Home Army, and that was all the guns there were.

—And you know who it was that was shouting? Rysia Hanin.

At the radio station in Kuybishev at that time she read the communiqués, poems, and appeals. She told me that it couldn't be ruled out that it was she who was encouraging you to struggle. . . . But they did not use weapons to jangle. Rysia Hanin says that over the radio nothing sounds as false as authentic sounds. . . .

—One day Anielewicz wanted to get one more gun. He killed a *werkschutz*, a German paramilitary guard, on Mila Street, and the same day in the afternoon the Germans came and as revenge pulled out every single person from the block of Zamenhofa between Mila Street and Muranowski Square, several hundred of them. We were furious at him. We even wanted to . . . Well, it doesn't matter.

In the house where they started taking people away, at the corner of Mila and Zamenhofa streets, lived my friend Hennoch Rus. (He was the one who'd prevailed in the decision about creating one armed organization in the Ghetto: the discussion had been going on for many hours and there had been several votes, but it was impossible to decide anything because each time there were the same number of votes in favor as against. In the end, it was finally Hennoch who changed his mind and raised his hand, the decision about creating the Jewish Combat Organization thereby being made.)

Hennoch Rus had had a little son. At the beginning of the war the boy got sick and a transfusion proved necessary, so I gave him some of my blood, but immediately after the transfusion, the kid died. It was probably because of the shock caused by the transfusion; it happens sometimes. Hennoch didn't say anything, but from that moment on he tended to steer clear of me: after all, it had been my blood that killed his child. Only, once the action started, he said to me: "Thanks to you my son died at home, like a human being. I am grateful to you."

We were accumulating weapons then.

We would smuggle them from the Aryan side (we were forcefully taking money from various institutions and private people); we also published newspapers, and our liaison girls took them all over Poland . . .

—How much did you have to pay for a revolver?

—Between three and fifteen thousand. The closer to April, the greater the cost: market demand was growing ever larger.

—And how much did you have to pay for hiding a Jew on the Aryan side?

—Two, five thousand. Different prices. It depended on whether the person looked Jewish, whether they had an accent, whether it was a man or a woman.

—That means that for the price of a single gun it would have been possible to hide one person for a month. Or perhaps two people, maybe even three.

—It was also possible with a gun to ransom a Jew from a *szmalcownik.**

Szmalcownik—a dark new "profession" that came into being during the war in Poland in which people would blackmail hiding Jews or the Poles who were helping to hide them—agreeing not to turn them in to the Gestapo for a fee.

—If you were then faced with a choice—one revolver or a single person's life for a month . . .

—We weren't ever faced with that kind of choice. Perhaps it's better that we weren't.

—Your courier girls took the newspapers all over Poland . . .

—One of them would smuggle them over to the Piotrkow Ghetto. In the Piotrkow Ghetto our people were in the community council, so there was an unusual degree of order there: there were no swindles, and the food and work were divided fairly. But we were very young and rigid in those days, and we believed that one shouldn't work in any of the community councils because that constituted collaboration with the enemy. So we ordered them to abandon that place, and a few of the people turned up in Warsaw, where it proved necessary to hide them because the Germans were out searching for all those council members from Piotrkow. I was supposed to take care of the Kellerman family. Two days before the conclusion of the liquidation action, as they were leading us from the Umschlagplatz to get the tickets, I saw Mr. Kellerman. He was standing behind the hospital door—it used to be a glass door, but the glass had been broken and the door had been covered over with wooden planks—and through a slit between these planks I saw his face. I signaled with my hand that I'd noticed him and would come back to get him—and then they took us away. I came back a couple of hours later, but nobody was behind that door any longer.

You know, I saw so many people dragged through the Umschlagplatz, both before that incident and after, but it's only toward those two that I would like to be able to explain myself—because I was supposed to take care of them, I told them I'd come back, right up till the last moment they must have been waiting for me, and I came too late.

—What about the liaison girl who used to travel to Piotr-kow?

—Oh, nothing. Once, on her way back, some Ukrainians caught her and were about to kill her, but our people some-how managed to pass them some money; the Ukrainians put her at the edge of a grave and shot her with blanks, she pretended to fall, and later she resumed carrying those news-papers.

We printed those newspapers on a duplicator. The machine was on Walowa Street, and one day we had to move it. On our way we met up with some Jewish policemen. We were carrying the machine, and they surrounded us and were about to cart us off to the Umschlagplatz. Their boss was a certain attorney who previously had been behaving impeccably, hadn't beaten anybody, and would feign that he didn't notice when people were escaping. Well, in this case we somehow managed to wrench ourselves free, and afterward I said to my friends, "Look, what a pig, after all." They excused it, explaining to me that he had probably been broken, that anyway this was probably the end both for us and for him. Later on, Maslanko said the same thing when the three of us were heading to West Germany to testify as witnesses. After the war I hadn't said a word to that attorney, but Maslanko said (we were having some drinks in that train): "What sense does it make to remember all that today?"

In fact. What sense—to remember?

A few days after the killing of the *werkschutz* and the massacre, in April, we were walking down the street—Antek, Anielewicz, and myself—and all of a sudden we came upon some of our own people in Muranowski Square. It was warm, a sunny day, and these folks had crawled out of their base-ments to be in the sun. "God," I said, "how can they possibly have come up? What are they doing that for?" And Antek, referring to me, muttered, "How much he must hate them, he would rather they stayed down there in the darkness. . . ." Because, as far as I was concerned, people were only supposed to come out during the night. If they came out in daylight, when they could be seen, it meant that they could die at any moment.

Antek, I remember, was the first one to predict during a meeting of the Command Group that the Germans would set the Ghetto on fire. When we were still pondering what to do, what kind of death to choose—whether to hurl ourselves at the walls, or to let ourselves be killed on the Citadel, or to set the Ghetto on fire and all of us burn together—Antek said, "What if they set the fire themselves?" We all said, "Don't talk nonsense. They wouldn't want to burn the whole town down." But on the second day of the uprising, they did indeed set a fire. We were in a shelter at that moment, and suddenly somebody burst in, desperately shouting that the place was on fire. Panic broke out. "That's it, the end, we're lost!" And that was the point where I had to slap this guy's face to calm him down.

We went out to the backyard, and they had indeed set fires all over, but luckily the central Ghetto wasn't burning yet, only our area, the Brush Factory, so I announced that we would have to break through the fire. Ania, that friend of Adam's who had managed to escape from Pawiak Prison, said she wasn't going to come because she had to stay with her mother. So we left her and scrambled across the backyard. Somehow we managed to reach the wall along Franciszkanska Street, where there was a breach in the wall, but it was lit up by a searchlight. People began to get hysterical all over again, how they couldn't possibly continue through there, how in that light we'd just get picked off one by one. And I said: "Suit yourselves, but then you're on your own." And they did stay behind, some six of them. Zygmunt provided cover, shooting at the searchlight with the only rifle we had, and we managed somehow to tear through. (Zygmunt was the guy who'd said that I would survive and he wouldn't and that I was supposed to find his daughter in Zamosc.)

You like this number with the searchlight, don't you? Better style than dying in a basement. One has more dignity leaping over a wall than suffocating to death in the dark, right?

—Sure.

—Then I can offer you something else in that style. Before the uprising, when the action in the little ghetto had just started, someone told me that they had taken Abrasza Blum away. He was an exceptionally thoughtful and wise man, our leader from before the war, so I went to see if I could find out what had happened with him.

I saw people arranged in ranks of four along Ciepla Street, and along both sides, every five, ten lines, there were Ukrainians. The street was cordoned off. I had to get in deeper, to see if I could spot Blum, but it was dangerous to walk behind the back of the Ukrainians or through the area where the crowd was standing because they might have raked me in as well. So I decided to walk between the Ukrainians and the crowd, so that everybody would see me. I walked real fast, very purposefully, as if I were simply entitled to be walking there. And you know what? Nobody even stopped me.

—I get the feeling that you yourself like stories of this kind—about fast, purposeful walks or shooting at searchlights—that you like them better than talking about basements.

—No.

—I think you do.

—Actually, I told you the story about the Ukrainians for quite a different reason. Because when I came back home that evening, there was Stasia, this girl with the long, thick braids, crying. "What are you crying about?" I asked her. "Because I thought they had taken you away."

That's all.

Everybody'd been busy with all their various important businesses, and Stasia had spent the whole day waiting for me to come back.

—We seemed to have dropped a stitch with that story about the searchlight. Although, to be honest, I am not at all sure that there is any particular thread to these conversations.

—Is that so bad?

—Of course not. We are not writing history, after all. We are writing about remembering. But let's get back to this searchlight: Zygmunt shot it out, you guys ran quickly. . . . Wait, what happened with Zygmunt's child in the convent at Zamosc?

—With Elzunia? I found her as soon as the war was over.

—Where is she now?

—She isn't anymore. She went to America. Some rich people adopted her and loved her a lot. She was beautiful and wise. And later she committed suicide.

—Why?

—I don't know. When I was in America, I went to see these parents. They showed me her bedroom. They hadn't changed a thing there since her death. But I still don't know why she did it.

—All the stories you tell, almost all of them, end with death.

—Really? That's because we're talking about *those* stories; that's the kind of story they are. The ones I tell about my patients end with life, after all.

—Zygmunt, Elzunia's father, shot the searchlight . . .

—. . . we jumped over the wall and ran into the central ghetto, Franciszkanska Street. And there, in the courtyard, were Blum (who, as it turned out, had not been taken away in that action after all) and Gepner.* The guy from whose suitcase I'd looted the red sweater. The one with the real, fluffy wool, that beautiful sweater . . .

—I know. Tosia recently sent you another one from Australia just exactly like it. And I have read a poem about Gepner: "Canto About an Iron Merchant, Abram Gepner." It says, among other things, that his friends on the Aryan side had implored him to get out, but he refused and stayed in the Ghetto till the end. Have you noticed how often in these stories that theme recurs: a chance to get out and the decision to stay? Korczak, Gepner, you guys . . . Maybe it's because making this decision between life and death afforded the last chance at preserving one's dignity. . . .

—Blum told us (in this courtyard in Franciszkanska Street) that there had been an assault by a group from the Home Army against the wall along Franciszkanska Street but that they'd failed and that Anielewicz was now a broken man, that there were no more arms, and that we couldn't count on getting any more. . . . I said, "All right, all right, let's not stand around here like this." And they asked, "Well, where shall we go, then?" There were more than thirty of us, and Gepner and Blum, and everybody was waiting for some kind of orders, and I didn't have a clue myself where to go.

For the time being, we went back down into the basements. And in the evening Adam said that he wanted to go back and get Ania. He asked me to give him a group of people; I asked if anyone wanted to go, and two or three people volunteered. They went there and later came back to say that that shelter with Ania and her mother had already been buried and that

---

*Gepner, the rich Jew of the first anecdote in this narrative, had somehow escaped after he and his family had been hauled out of their basement, so that he resurfaces here.

those six guys who hadn't wanted to come along with us at the searchlight were also dead.

Perhaps you want to ask me whether I have a guilty conscience over how I left them behind?

—I don't want to.

—No, I don't feel guilty, no. But I do feel sorry about it all the time.

And the next day we joined up with everybody: Anielewicz, Celina, Jurek Wilner. We got to their bunker. Those girls, these two prostitutes, prepared something for us to eat and Guta handed out cigarettes. It was a good, quiet day.

What do you think, can one tell the people about things like that?

—What do you mean?

—About those guys I left in the backyard?

Should a doctor tell people about such things? After all, in medicine, every life, every chance, even the smallest chance at saving life, counts.

—Maybe instead we should talk about the searchlight, about leaping over the wall, that sort of thing?

—But everything alternates, you see. You run somewhere, then someone gets killed, then you run again, then Adam sticks his head out of the basement and a grenade begins to roll along the molding, and I yell "Adam, a grenade!" and the grenade explodes right on top of his head. Then I jump out of the basement, there are some Germans in the backyard but I have these two guns, you know, the ones with the two crisscrossing belts, I shoot . . .

—And you manage to hit with both of them?

—Of course not, I don't hit with either of them, but I do manage to get to the building, and the soldiers come running after me, so I run onto the roof—is this the right kind of story?

—Excellent. First rate.

—Do you think it is prettier to run along a roof than to sit in a basement?

—I prefer it when you're running along the roofs.

—I didn't see any difference then. But I saw it later, in the general Warsaw uprising, in 1944, when everything was already happening during the day, in sunlight, in open spaces without walls. We were able to attack, to withdraw, to run. The Germans were shooting, but I was shooting, too, I had my own rifle, a white-and-red armband, there were other people around with white-and-red armbands—lots of people—listen, what a terrific, congenial fight that was!

—Shall we get back to the roof?

—I ran on the roof over to another building. All that in this red sweater, and a red sweater like that on a roof makes an excellent target. But it was difficult to shoot into the sun, so that I was hard to hit. In this other building there turned out to be a young guy lying on a big sack of biscuits.

I stopped and hid alongside this guy. He gave me one biscuit, then another one, but then he didn't want to give me anymore. It was noon. By about 6 P.M. the guy had died, and I had the sackful of biscuits all to myself. Unfortunately, it is difficult to jump with a sack, and I later had to jump again. When I eventually got out to the backyard, there were five of our boys lying there killed. One of them was named Stasiek. That very morning he had asked me for an address on the other side, and I'd told him, "Not yet, it's too early." And he'd been saying: "But this *is* the end, give me that address, please." And I didn't have any address. A moment later he'd jumped out into the backyard, and now I'd found him again.

It was necessary to bury these guys.

We dug the grave in the courtyard at 30 Franciszkanska Street. It is a tremendous job to dig a grave for five people. We buried them and, since it was May 1st, we sang over their grave in very low voices the first verse of "The Internationale." Can you believe that? One had to be totally out of one's mind to sing in a courtyard on Franciszkanska Street.

Later, we managed to get some sugar and we were drinking sweet water. At that point I happened to have a small rebellion in my group. These rebels thought that I was being unfair with them, not giving them enough weapons, so they organized a hunger strike against me: they refused to drink this water.

You know what the worst part of it was?

How more and more people were waiting for me to order them what to do next.

—How did the strike end? (A hunger strike in the Ghetto, good God!)

—As usual with such things: they were forced to drink that water. Don't you know how you force people to do things during a war?

So more and more people, older than me and more experienced, were asking me what to do and I didn't have a clue myself. I felt absolutely alone.

That entire day as I'd lain there next to that guy who was dying on his biscuits, this had been the only thing on my mind.

On May 6th, Anielewicz and Mira came to us. We were supposed to have some kind of meeting, but actually there was nothing to talk about anymore, so he went to sleep. And so did I. The next morning I said, "Stay with us. What are you going back for?" But he wanted to go. We saw them off and the day after that, the eighth, we went to their bunker at 18 Mila Street (it was night already), and we shouted—but nobody answered. Finally some guy said: "They don't exist anymore. They all committed suicide." A few people were still left and those two girls, the prostitutes. We took them with us, and the moment we got back to our place it turned out that Kazik from the Aryan side was already there with the sewermen and that we were going to be heading out. (The two girls asked whether they could join us. I said no.) Our guides through the sewers had been sent by Jozwiak—"Witold" from the Polish Workers' Party. They led us through the sewers to a manhole under Prosta Street, where we waited a night, and a day, and then another night, and finally, on May 10th at ten in the morning, the hatch was lifted, a car was waiting with our people and "Krzaczek" who'd been sent by "Witold." A crowd of people was standing around, looking at us with horror. We were dark and dirty, with weapons—there was total silence as we clambered out into the blinding light of May.

Andrzej Wajda would like to make a movie about the Ghetto. He says he would use some footage from the archives and have Edelman tell the whole story in front of the camera.

He would be speaking at the places where the events he was describing had actually taken place.

For instance, next to the bunker at 18 Mila Street (today snow lay there and little boys were sledding).

Or at the entrance to the Umschlagplatz, next to the gate.

The gate, by the way, does not exist anymore. The old wall collapsed while the Inflancka housing project was under construction. Now several tall gray buildings rise there—exactly along what used to be the loading platform. My friend Anna Stronska lives in one of those buildings. I tell her how just outside her kitchen window the last cars of the train once stood, because the engine car was just over there by the poplars. Stronska, who has a heart problem, grows pale.

"Listen," she says. "I was always good to them. The ghosts wouldn't harm me, would they?"

"Of course not," I say. "They'll only protect you, you'll see."

"You think so?" asks Stronska, and she relaxes a bit.

So when they were tidying up after the construction, the old wall collapsed, but a new one, made of healthy white bricks, was quickly erected in the very same place. Commemorative plaques and candle holders were slotted in, and little green flower boxes were hung, and grass was planted all around, and very soon everything was tidy, neat, and new.

Or, for instance, Wajda might use the monument.

On April 19th, the day of the anniversary, the Orbis state tourist buses would arrive as usual with their foreign guests, and ladies in spring suits and men with cameras would get off these buses. All over the park, old women sitting with baby carriages would stare at the buses and the delegations from factories ready to lay wreaths. "In our basement," one of the women would say, "one of them was hiding under the coal and it was necessary to pass her food through a little window from the street." (It might also happen that the one to whom they had been passing the food would be standing now in a spring suit, brought by a tour bus.) Later, there would be the sound of drums, and the delegations with wreaths would move on; after the delegations some private people would start to approach, with little bunches of flowers in their hands or with one yellow jonquil, and after everything, after the snare drums and the flowers, an old man with a white beard would emerge suddenly from the crowd and would start reciting the Kaddish. He would stand at the foot of the monument, below the burning torches, and with a breaking voice he would start to chant his plaintive prayer. For six million dead. Such a lonely old man, in a long black coat.

74

The crowd would mingle. "Marek," someone would shout, "how are you?!" "Marysia, you always look so young," he would declare happily, because it would be Marysia Sawicka, the same girl who before the war used to run the eight hundred meters at the Skra sports club along with Michal Klepfisz's sister, and who later hid this sister-runner at her place, along with Michal's wife, and his daughter. . . .

The daughter and the wife survived, and Michal, who stayed behind at Bonifraterska Street, in that attic where he covered a machine gun with his body so that the others could pass— he has a symbolic grave in the Jewish cemetery with an inscription that reads:

ENGINEER MICHAL KLEPFISZ
4/17/1913–4/20/1943

That would probably be the next place for Wajda to train his cameras.

Nearby there is Jurek Blones's grave, his twenty-year-old sister Guta's, and their twelve-year-old brother Lusiek's, and then Fajgele Goldsztajn's (which one was she, Marek does not even remember her face), and Zygmunt Frydrych's, Elzunia's father who'd told him that first day, "You will survive, but remember: in Zamosc, in a convent . . ."

In this case, it's not a symbolic grave:

After that group had escaped through the sewers, they'd been driven to Zielonka, where a hideaway had been prepared for them, but ten minutes later, the Germans had arrived. They were buried in Zielonka, next to a fence, so that it was easy to find their bodies after the war.

Another group lies a few hundred feet farther on, deeper along the path, having been brought there after the war from near the Bug River. After they'd clambered out of the sewers, they were supposed to have headed east to cross the river and join the partisans, but they'd been fired on while still in the middle of the river. (They'd climbed out of the sewers at Prosta Street. The manhole cover suddenly opened, and "Krzaczek" was already yelling "Out! Out!" but eight people were missing. Edelman had ordered those eight to head over to a wider sewer, because having waited throughout a night and day and into another night underneath that closed-off manhole cover, they'd been beginning to asphyxiate and die owing to the water reeking of feces and methane. Now, with the cover up, Edelman ordered someone to call them and bring them back, but nobody moved. Nobody wanted to move away from the outlet, the cover having now been lifted open, all that fresh air and light pouring in; they could already hear the voices of the people who had come to rescue them. Edelman then told Szlamek Szuster to run and fetch the others, and he did. But up there it was "Krzaczek" and Kazik who were in charge of everything, and they were yelling that they had to drive off immediately, that there would be another truck, and despite the fact that Celina pulled out her revolver and shouted "Stop or I'll shoot!" the truck drove off. This emergence from the sewers had been organized by Kazik. He was nineteen years old at the time, and what he accomplished was truly extraordinary, only that now he calls Marek sometimes from a city three thousand kilometers away and says that it was all his fault, because he didn't force "Krzaczek" to wait. To which Edelman answers that that's not true, that Kazik performed marvelously, and that the only one responsible was he himself, since it was he who told the others to move away from the outlet in the first place. At which point Kazik, still from his city three thousand kilometers away, says, "Stop it. After all, it's the Germans who were responsible." And he adds: "Why is it that ever since that time nobody asks me about those who survived? They always ask only about the dead." The manhole cover, which is in Prosta Street,

76

in what is now the Za Zelazna Brama housing project, would also do as a location for Wajda's film.)

At the very end of the cemetery path, where the graves end and some sort of a field begins—a flat field with high grass, spreading out toward Powazkowska Street, right up to the wall—there aren't any plaques at all anymore. Here lie all those who died before the final liquidation of the Ghetto— the ones who starved to death, who died of typhoid or of exhaustion, in the streets, in deserted apartments. Every morning the laborers from the Eternity Company would go out with their pushcarts and collect the bodies, placing them one on top of the next in piles on the carts, and finally they'd cross Okopowa Street, enter the cemetery (which was on the Aryan side), and trudge right this way, along this path, toward that wall.

At first, they buried the corpses alongside the wall, but then, as the influx of the bodies swelled, they gradually over- flowed into the interior of the cemetery, until the entire field was filled.

Over the graves of Michal Klepfisz, Abrasza Blum, and the others killed in Zielonka, there stands a monument: an up- right man with a rifle in one hand, a grenade upraised in the other one, he has a cartridge pouch sashed about his waist, a bag with maps at his side, and a belt across his chest. None of them had ever looked like this: they didn't have rifles, cartridge pouches, or maps; besides, they were dark and dirty. But in the monument they look the way they were ideally supposed to. On the monument, everything is bright and beautiful.

Next to Abrasza Blum lies his wife, Luba, the one who was the head of the nurses' college in the Ghetto. She got five life tickets for her school, and there were sixty students; so she said: "These should go to the ones with the best grades in nursing"—and she had them answer a single question:

"Describe the appropriate nursing care for a patient during the first days following a heart attack." The five students who answered best got the tickets.

After the war Luba Blum ran an orphanage. Children found in closets, convents, coal trunks, and cemetery vaults were brought to her orphanage. These kids were subsequently shaved bald, dressed in clothes from the United Nations Relief and Rehabilitation Administration, taught to play piano and how they shouldn't smack while eating. One of the girls had been born after her mother was raped by Germans and kids kept calling her "Kraut." Another one was completely bald, because all her hair had fallen out due to lack of vitamins. A third one, who had been hiding out in the countryside, had to be asked several times by her teacher not to keep telling everyone what the peasants would do with her in the attic, since proper little ladies were not supposed to tell such stories in society.

Luba Blum, who in the Ghetto used to make sure that all her students wore the cleanest possible starched bonnets, and in the orphanage used to instruct all her wards that they should politely answer, and in full sentences, all the questions put to them by the visiting gentlemen, questions about how and in what manner their daddies had been killed, because these gentlemen would presently return to America and later on send packages, lots of packages with dresses and halvah— Luba Blum today lies on the main, orderly path. If one diverges slightly into the interior of the cemetery, there is an increasingly dense thicket of twigs, broken columns, overgrown graves, plaques—eighteen hundred . . . nineteen hundred thirty . . . citizen of Praga . . . doctor at law . . . the bereaved—traces of a world that must actually have existed once upon a time.

Along a side path, "Engineer Adam Czerniakow, Chairman of the Warsaw Ghetto, died on July 23, 1942," and a

78

fragment of Norwid's poem on Mickiewicz's death: "So that it little matters in what urn you rest, / Because they will open your grave again someday, /And assess your merits differently." ("This is the only thing we reproach him for: that he made his death his own private business.")

A funeral. It proceeds along an ordered, busy path, several people, wreaths, sashes (from the pensioners' club, from the local union cell . . .). An elderly man approaches everyone and, discreetly whispering, asks, "Excuse me, are you perhaps Jewish?"—and continuing on—"Excuse me, are you . . . ?" He needs to have ten Jews in order to recite the Kaddish over the coffin, and he's managed to gather only seven.

"In this crowd?"

"You can see for yourself, madam, I am asking everybody, and it always ends up being seven."

He counts them out on his meticulously extended fingers: seven, in the entire cemetery, the *Jewish* cemetery. It is impossible even to recite the Kaddish.

The Jews are at the Umschlagplatz, in Stronska's apartment, at the loading platform.

Bearded, in gaberdines, yarmulkes, some of them in hats bordered with red fox fur, two of them even in *maciejowkas** . . . Crowds, throngs of Jews: on shelves, tables, above the couch, along the walls . . .

My friend Anna Stronska collects folk art, and the folk artists like to recreate their neighbors from before the war.

Stronska collects her Jews from everywhere, from all over Poland—from Przemysl, where they sell her the most beautiful pieces and give her the best price because her father was a foreman there before the war; from the Kielce area; but the most valuable are those from Krakow. On the second day of

---

Maciejowkas, the visored caps emblematic of Marshal Jozef Pilsudski's legions.

Easter, in front of Norbetanki Church in Salwator, there is an annual church fair, and only there can one still get the Jews in their black robes and white satin tallithim, the tefillin on their heads, everything arrayed just so, according to the rules, exactly as it should be.

They cluster in groups. Figurines.

Some of them gesticulate animatedly in the midst of lively conversations; nearby, one fellow reads a paper, but the other group has been talking so loudly that he's raised his eyes from the page and is now listening in. A few are praying. Two men in reddish robes are splitting their sides with laughter for some reason; an elderly man with a stick and a little suitcase passes by: perhaps a doctor?

Everybody is busy and involved with something, because they are *those* Jews, from before everything. So I bring Edelman to Stronska's, to let him see those Jews from the normal time, and as we are about to leave, Stronska reports that a neighbor who lives a few blocks away, on Mila Street, keeps telling her about an eerie dream.

This neighbor has been dreaming this same dream, every night, ever since the day she moved into that apartment. Actually, she is not entirely sure that it's a dream, because she dreams that she's awake and just lying there in her room, only it seems not quite to be her room. There is old furniture in it, a huge stove, a window in a blind wall. And because she returns here every night, she has gotten used to all the pieces of furniture and is already able to recognize trinkets left on the armchairs and the dresser. Sometimes she is visited by a feeling that behind the door there is somebody. This sensation of somebody's presence becomes so strong that sometimes she gets up and checks whether it isn't a thief— but no, nobody is there.

One night she sees herself once again in this room of hers—no, not her room. Everything is in its usual place: the stoves, the trinkets on the dresser. And then, all of a sudden, the door opens and a young woman, a Jew, enters the room.

She approaches the bed.

She stops.

They look at each other intently. Neither of them says a word, but it is obvious what they would like to say. The young woman stares: "Oh, so it's you here . . ." And the other one, the dreamer, starts explaining—that the building is new, that she was, after all, assigned this apartment. . . . The young woman makes a calming gesture: everything is all right, she just wanted to see who was here now, simple curiosity . . . and she drifts over to the window and casts herself out to the street below from the fifth floor.

From the night of this variation, the dream has never again recurred, and that sensation of somebody else's presence has likewise disappeared.

So that it's precisely in places like this, and in many others, that Wajda might shoot his movie. Only Edelman says that he would not utter a single word before Wajda's cameras, because he could tell it all only once.

And he has told it.

Why did you become a doctor?

—Because I had to continue doing what I was doing before, in the Ghetto. In the Ghetto we made the decision for forty thousand people—there were forty thousand of them left in April 1943. We decided that they would not voluntarily collaborate in their own deaths. As a doctor I could continue to be responsible for the life of at least one person—so I became a doctor.

You would have liked me to answer like this, right? It would have sounded good? But it didn't quite happen like that. What happened was that the war ended. The war—a victory for everybody. Only for me it was a lost war, and all the time I was haunted by a feeling that I still had something to do, somewhere to go, that somebody was still counting on me and I had to go rescue him. Something seemed to propel me from one town to another and from country to country, but when I'd arrive, it would turn out that nobody was waiting, that there wasn't anybody counting on me for help anymore, and that, in general, there was nothing more to do. So I came back (people kept asking me, "Do you want to look at those walls again, those empty streets?" and I knew that yes, indeed, I had to come back here and look at them). So I came back and I lay in bed and simply stayed like that. I slept. I slept for days and weeks. From time to time friends would wake me up and tell me that, after all, seriously, I had to do something about myself. For a while, it seemed to me I might study economics. I don't remember why anymore. But finally Ala registered me in medical school.

Ala was already my wife. I'd met her when she came with a patrol organized by Dr. Swital from the Home Army to lead us out of a bunker in the Zoliborz district. We'd been left there, on Promyka Street, after the general Warsaw uprising in 1944—Antek, Celina, Tosia Goliborska, and I, among others—and in November they sent this patrol around to fetch us. (Promyka Street runs along the Vistula River, so it was still the front line, and everything was mined. I remember Ala's taking her shoes off and crossing the mine field barefoot, because she imagined that if she happened to step on a mine barefoot, for some reason it wouldn't go off.)

As I was saying, Ala registered me in medical school, so I

started going there. But I wasn't the least bit interested, and when we'd get back home, I would throw myself back onto the bed. Everybody else was studying assiduously, and because I was lying there with my face to the wall all the time, some of my friends began drawing things for me on this wall, so that at least I would be memorizing something. One day, for instance, they would draw a stomach, another day a heart—always with great precision, by the way, you know, the ventricles, the auricles, the aorta. . . .

Things continued more or less like this for about two years. Occasionally people would call and invite me to participate in a panel discussion about the Ghetto . . .

—You'd already acquired hero status?

—Sort of. Or they would come by and say: "Mr. Edelman, please tell us, tell us how it was." But I was rather subdued, and I tended to prove rather pale and ineffectual on those panels.

Do you know what I remember best from this period?

Mikolaj's death. The one who was a member of the Zegota (the Council to Aid the Jews) as a representative of our underground.

Mikolaj got sick and died.

He died—Hanna, do you understand?—normally, in a hospital, *in bed*! He was the first of the people I knew who simply died and was not killed. The day before, I'd visited him in the hospital and he said: "Mr. Marek, should anything happen to me, here, under the pillow is the notebook and everything is accounted for there, to the last penny. Folks may ask about it one day, so please, remember that it's all balanced and there is even a slight surplus."

Can you imagine, Hanna, what he had there? It was a thick notebook with a black cover in which throughout the whole war he'd been recording how he was spending all the dollars. The dollars we'd received in the drops to buy arms. Almost a hundred was left, and the bank notes were all there in the back of the notebook.

—Did you give the cash and the notebook to those union leaders in America, those hosts who seemed so profoundly moved in 1963?

—You know, I didn't even take this notebook from the hospital. I told Antek and Celina about it and—I remember—we laughed a lot about the whole thing, about the notebook and how Mikolaj was dying in such a bizarre way, you know, lying between clean sheets, in bed. We almost split our sides laughing, and Celina finally had to remind us that, after all, such behavior was slightly improper.

—Did your friends eventually stop having to draw those hearts on the wall?

—Yes.

One day I happened to pop in during some lecture—probably only to get some forms signed—but I heard a professor say: "When a doctor knows what his patient's eyes look like, and his skin, and his tongue, he should be able to tell what's wrong with him." I liked that. I realized that a patient's illness is like a puzzle and if one put the pieces together correctly, one should know what's going on inside that patient.

From that moment I took up medicine, and from then on the stuff you were wanting me to say at the outset applies. But I only understood it much, much later: how by being a doctor I could continue to be responsible for human life.

—Why actually do you feel you have to be responsible for human life?

—Probably because everything else seems to me less important.

—Perhaps it was a question of your having been twenty then? If one has lived the most important moments of one's life by the age of twenty, afterward it can get rather difficult finding an equally significant job . . .

—You know, Hanna, in the clinic where I later worked, there was a big, tall palm tree there in the hall. I would stand underneath that palm tree sometimes—and I'd look out over the rooms where my patients were lying. This was a long time ago, when we didn't yet have today's medications or operations or devices available, and the majority of the people in those rooms were in effect simply condemned to death. My assignment was to save as many as possible—and I realized, that day under the palm, that actually it was the same assignment as I'd had there, at the Umschlagplatz. There, too, I would stand at the gate and pull out individuals from the throngs of those condemned to die.

—And all your life you have been standing at this gate, right?

—Actually, yes. And when I can't accomplish anything else, there is always one thing left: to assure them the most comfortable death possible. So that they might not know, not suffer, not be afraid. So that they need not humiliate themselves.

You have to provide them with a way of dying such that they don't become like *those*—the ones from the fourth floor at the Umschlagplatz.

—People have told me, Marek, that when you're taking care of simple and not terribly serious cases, you do it in a way out of a sense of duty, that you only really light up when the game begins, when the race with death begins.

—This is, after all, my role.

God is trying to blow out the candle and I'm quickly trying to shield the flame, taking advantage of His brief inattention. To keep the flame flickering, even if only for a little while longer than He would wish.

It is important: He is not terribly just. It can also be very satisfying, because whenever something does work out, it means you have, after all, fooled Him . . .

—A race with God? How delicious!

—You know, when you've had to see all those people off on the trains, later on you can have some things to settle with Him. And they all passed by me because I stood there by that gate from the first day till the last. All of them. Four hundred thousand people passed right by me.

Of course, every life ends in the same way, but what counts is postponing the sentence for eight, ten, or fifteen years. That's not nothing. When, thanks to that ticket, Mrs. Tenenbaum's daughter lived those extra three months—that was a lot because she managed to get to know love during those three months. And the girls we cure of stenosis or of narrowed valves, they have time to grow up and make love and have babies—then how much more do they manage to live than Mrs. Tenenbaum's daughter?

I had such a nine-year-old girl once, Urszula, with contraction of the dual lung valve; she was spitting pink, foamy sputum, and suffocating—but at that time we weren't yet operating on children. For that matter, they were only then just beginning to operate on heart defects in Poland at all. But she was already dying, so I called the Professor and told him that this little one was going to suffocate at any moment. He flew up within a few hours and he operated on her that very day. She quickly got better, left the hospital, graduated. . . . Over the years she's come to visit us from time to time, once with a husband, later divorced, pretty, tall, with dark hair. Before she used to be slightly disfigured by a squint, but we got her an operation with a very good ophthalmologist and her eyes are all right now.

Then we had Teresa with a heart defect, swollen like a barrel, dying. After we'd operated and the swelling had subsided, she immediately demanded, "Send me home." It was strange because during all that time, nobody from her home had ever come to see her. I went there. It was a back room with a concrete floor. She lived with a sick mother and two younger sisters. She said she had to go home because someone had to take care of those sisters—she was ten at that time—and she went. She later had a baby. After the labor we had to pull her out of lung swelling, but as soon as she could breathe, she said she had to leave to take care of her baby. Sometimes she comes to us and says she has everything she's ever wanted to have—a home, a baby, a husband, and what's most important, she says, she's escaped that tiny room at the back of a store.

Later we had Grazyna from the orphanage, whose alcoholic father died in a mental hospital and whose mother died of TB. I used to tell her she should never have a baby, but she's gone ahead and had one and she's coming back to us with circulatory system asthenia. She's getting weaker and weaker, she can't work anymore, she can't hold this baby anymore, but she puts him in a stroller, proud that she has had a baby like any normal woman. Her husband loves her a lot and won't consent to an operation. We don't have the courage to insist, so Grazyna is slowly fading.

Maybe I am getting some of this wrong, but I don't remember all of them clearly anymore. It's strange. When they are here—when you're having to help them—they become your closest people in the world, and you know everything about them. You know that this one has a concrete floor at home; that this other one's father drinks and her mother is mentally ill; that this third one has problems with mathematics at school; and that this fourth one's husband is not good for her at all; or that there are exams at college right now so that it's necessary to get a cab to take this new one together with a nurse and medication to that exam. And you also know all about their hearts: that the withdrawal from their various valves is either too narrow or too wide (if it is too narrow there is ischemia—if it's too wide, there is blood stasis and the blood doesn't make it through the circuit). You look at a patient, and when she is so pretty, skinny, with pink complexion, it means that she developed peripheral blood stasis and it resulted in dilatation of capillary blood vessels; or if she is pale and her blood vessels in her neck throb, her aorta outlet is too wide. . . . You know all about them, and they are your closest people during those few days of mortal danger. And then they get better. They leave for their homes, you forget their faces, somebody new arrives, and already this new person alone is the most important.

A few days ago they brought in a seventy-year-old lady with asthenia. The Professor operated on her. It was a really risky operation—an acute circulation asthenia. As she was falling asleep, she was praying. "God," she said, "bless the hands of the Professor and the thoughts of the doctors from Pirogow."

The doctors from Pirogow—that's us, me and Aga Zuchowska.

Well, tell me, to whom else but my patient—a little old lady—would it occur to pray *for my thoughts*?

Isn't it high time already we put a little bit of order here? After all, people are expecting numbers from us, dates, data about soldiers and their weapons. People are very strongly attached to the importance of historical facts and chronology.

For instance: there were 220 insurgents, 2090 Germans.

The Germans have their air force, artillery, armored vehicles, flamethrowers, 82 machine guns, 135 submachine guns, 1358 rifles. Each insurgent, according to the report of the uprising commander's deputy, has one pistol, five grenades, and five incendiary bottles. There are three rifles in each area. For the entire Ghetto, there are only two mines and one submachine gun.

The Germans enter on April 19th at 4 A.M. The first battles occur on Muranowski Square, Zamenhofa and Gesia streets. At 2 P.M. the Germans withdraw without having taken a single person to the Umschlagplatz. ("At that point we believed it was very important that they hadn't been able to take anybody away that day. We even considered it a victory.")

April 20th: there are no Germans at all till past noon (for a full twenty-four hours there has not been a single German in the Ghetto!); they return at 2 P.M. They approach the Brush Factory area. They're trying to open the gate. A mine explodes, they withdraw. (This is one of the two mines in the Ghetto. The other one, on Nowolipie Street, never goes off.) They force their way into the attic. Michal Klepfisz smothers a German machine gun with his body, the group manages to get through—the radio station Dawn will presently broadcast the news that Michal had fallen on the field of glory and read General Sikorski's order awarding him the Virtuti Military Cross, fifth class.

Now comes the scene with the three SS officers. Wearing white rosettes and with their machine guns pointed down, they propose a truce and a removal of the wounded. The insurgents shoot at the officers, but they fail to hit any of them.

In the American author John Hersey's book *The Wall*, this scene is described in great detail.

Felix, one of the imaginary characters, reports it with ambivalence and embarrassment. There is still in him, the author points out, a longing, so typical in the Western tradition, for rules of warfare, a need to honor a basic sense of "fair play," even in a deadly struggle. . . .

It was Zygmunt who shot at the SS men. They had only one rifle and Zygmunt was the best shot because he'd managed to put in some actual military service before the war. Seeing the approaching officers with their white rosettes, Edelman had said, "Fire," and Zygmunt had fired.

Edelman is the only survivor from among all the people who participated in that scene—at any rate, on the insurgents' side. I ask him whether he felt embarrassed violating the rules of war, that basic sense of "fair play" so typical of the Western tradition.

He says he felt no embarrassment whatsoever, because those three Germans were exactly the same fellows who had already transported four hundred thousand people to the Treblinka camp, only now they happened to be wearing the white rosettes . . .

(In his report, Stroop mentioned those "parliamentarians" and the "bandits" who fired on them.

Soon after the war Edelman encountered Stroop.

The prosecutor's office and the Commission to Investigate Nazi Crimes asked him to help determine some particulars in a confrontation with Stroop: whether there was a wall in a particular place, whether there was a gate, a few topographical details.

They were sitting at a table—the prosecutor, the Commission's representative, and he—and a tall, cleanly shaven man in shiny boots was escorted into the room. He came to attention before them. "I also rose. The prosecutor told Stroop who I was. Stroop drew himself up, clicked his heels, and turned his head toward me. In the military, they call this 'rendering military honors' or something like that. I was asked whether I'd seen him kill people. I answered that I had never seen this man before, that I was seeing him for the first time. Later, they asked me whether it was possible that there was a gate at such-and-such a place and that the tanks had approached from that direction, because this was what Stroop was declaring and it didn't seem to fit in. I said: 'It's possible that there was a gate there and that the tanks came from there.' I felt sorry. This man was standing before me at attention, without his belt; he had already received one death sentence. What difference did it make where the wall was and where the gate? I just wanted to leave that room as quickly as possible.")

The parliamentarians leave (Zygmunt, unfortunately, missed), and in the evening everybody goes down to the basements.

During the night a boy runs in shouting that there is fire. Panic breaks out. . . .

Excuse me. "A boy runs in shouting . . ." We don't need that density of detail for a serious historical report. Nor do we need the fact that, after the boy's shout, a few thousand people started to panic, which extinguished the candles so that it became necessary quickly to reprimand the boy. All of this is too thorough for History. . . . Well, at any rate, after a moment people begin to calm down: they can see that someone is taking charge. ("People should always have this sense that someone is in charge here.")

So the Germans are beginning to set the Ghetto on fire. The Brush Factory area is already in flames. It is necessary to break through these flames into the central ghetto.

When a building is burning, at first the floors burn, and then burning posts begin to fall from above, but between the first falling post and the next one, a few minutes pass, and this is when one should run. It is terribly hot: broken glass and asphalt melt under one's feet. People are running through the flames between those falling posts. A wall. A hole in the wall with a searchlight trained on it. "We are not going."

"So, stay here." A shot into the searchlight, the people are running. A backyard, six guys, shooting, running. Five guys, a grave, Stasiek, Adam, "The Internationale." . . .

One more thing: that same day when they dug the grave and softly sang the first verse of "The Internationale," they had had to make their way through basements to another building. Four men went down to dig an opening while upstairs the Germans started throwing grenades into the basement. Smoke and poison gas began to penetrate through, and Edelman ordered them to seal up the opening. There was still one guy left on the other side, but people were beginning to suffocate and it was impossible to wait for him.

And here we have a strict chronology. We know already that the first one to die was Michal Klepfisz, then those six guys, then the five guys, then Stasiek, then Adam, and then the guy who'd had to be buried. And then several hundred people in the shelter. But this happened later, when the whole Ghetto was on fire and everybody had moved into the basements. "It was terribly hot there and some woman had let her child go out for a moment; the Germans gave him a candy, asking him, 'And where is your mom?' and the kid led them back so that the Germans then blew up the whole shelter, several hundred people. Some of us later felt that we should have shot this kid the moment he got out. But this wouldn't have helped any, because the Germans had sound-detection devices and were using them to track down the people in the basements."

So this is the chronology of the events.

Historical order turns out to be nothing more than the order of dying.

History is happening on the other side of the wall, where the reports are being written, radio announcements are being sent to the world, and help is being demanded from the world. Any expert today knows the texts of the cables and governmental communications. But who knows about the boy who had to be buried because poisonous gas was penetrating into the basement? Who today knows about that boy?

These reports are being written on the Aryan side by "Waclaw." For example: "Communiqué #3. Wac. A/9, April 21: Jewish Combat Organization directing the struggle of the Warsaw Ghetto rejected a German ultimatum to throw down their arms by 10 A.M. Tuesday. . . . The Germans deployed artillery, tanks, and armored brigades. The state of siege of the Ghetto and the struggle of the Jewish militants are virtually the sole subject of conversation in this city of a million people. . . ."

"Waclaw" had previously broadcast information about the Ghetto liquidation action, and it was precisely from him the world learned about the existence of the Umschlagplatz, about the transports, the gas chambers, and the Treblinka camp. "Waclaw"—Henryk Wolinski—who has been mentioned in every account of the Ghetto, was the head of the Jewish Department of the Chief Command of the Home Army. He was the liaison between the ZOB (the Jewish Combat Organization) and the Command of the AK (the Home Army). Among other things, he transmitted to the chief commander the first declaration of the creation of the ZOB, and to Jurek Wilner, Home Army Commander Grot-Rowecki's order subordinating the ZOB to the Home Army. He put the Jews in touch with Colonel Monter and the other officers who later supplied them with arms and taught them how to use them. In most cases, the teacher was Zbigniew Lewandowski— "Szyna"—the head of the Technical Research Office of the Home Army. Today Dr. Lewandowski says that only two people from the Ghetto attended those "classes," a man and a woman; at the beginning he was concerned about this, but it quickly became evident that the man was a chemist and he was catching on to everything very fast and passing the instructions on to his friends in the Ghetto. In addition to instructions, they also received potassium chlorate, to which they could themselves add sulfuric acid, gasoline, paper, sugar, and glue to make ignition bottles. "Molotov cocktails?" I ask to make sure, but Dr. Lewandowski huffs: "You can't even compare them. Our bottles were delicate, sophisticated, covered over with this chlorate and wrapped in paper, and the ignition points went around the whole surface. Really, a sophisticated, elegant item: the newest achievement of the Home Army's Technical Research Office. In general, everything we were giving to the ZOB—the bottles, the people, the arms— were the best available to us at the time."

Up till today Dr. Lewandowski hasn't known the name of that man who'd come to his place at 62 Marszalkowska Street (first floor, in the backyard to the left). "He was a tall man, with brown hair," he says. "Not one of those aggressive types, those 'pistols'; rather, silent and quiet. But," the doctor adds, "in particularly dangerous actions the 'pistols' were seldom the best, but rather the inconspicuous ones."

So I tell the doctor that the man he had been teaching was Michal Klepfisz.

Together with Stanislaw Herbst, "Waclaw" described the first big liquidation action in the Ghetto, and this report, in the form of a microfilm, was transmitted by a courier via Paris and Lisbon, such that just before Christmas Eve, 1942, General Sikorski confirmed having received it. Jurek Wilner, the ZOB's representative on the Aryan side, brought news from the Ghetto every day, thanks to which the reports were updated and current information could be broadcast to London all the time. For instance:

An atmosphere of crazy panic: the action is supposed to start at 6:30 and everybody is prepared that he or she can be taken away at any moment, from any place . . .

The last phase of the liquidation started on Sunday. At 10 o'clock that morning, all Jews were required to be in front of the Jewish Council building. There they started to distribute life tickets. Everybody is required to wear them on their chests. They consist of yellowish chits of paper with a handwritten number, the Jewish Council seal, and a signature. The tickets don't have names . . .

Last week at the Umschlagplatz people were paying 1000 (1 thousand) zlotys for 1 kilogram of bread, 3 zlotys for a cigarette.

When the gendarmes came to take him, Seweryn Majde threw a heavy ashtray at one of them, hitting him on his head. Majde was obviously executed. This has been the only known case of intentional self-defense . . .

Travelers going through Treblinka have observed that the trains don't stop at this station.

Every day like that: Wilner brings information from the Ghetto, "Waclaw" writes the reports, radio operators transmit them to London, and the London radio—contrary to its practice heretofore—does not include any information about the matter in its programming. The clandestine radio operators back in Poland, at the insistence of their bosses, ask the reason, but the BBC remains silent. Only after a month does it include in its information service the first news about the ten thousand people a day and about the Umschlagplatz. Because—as it turns out later—all along London has not been believing "Waclaw's" reports. "We thought that you were exaggerating a little with all that anti-German propaganda . . . ," they explain, once they get confirmation from their own sources. . . . So Jurek Wilner would smuggle out from the Ghetto, alongside the news, additional texts for telegrams, like the one to be sent to the Jewish Congress in the United States, which ended with the following lines: "Brothers! The remaining Jews in Poland live convinced that in the most horrible days in our history you did not lend us your help. Say something. This is our last appeal to you."

In April 1943 "Waclaw" delivers to the ZOB Command Group's Antek a dispatch from Colonel Monter "welcoming the armed action of the Warsaw Jews" and subsequently informs him that the Home Army will try to break through the Ghetto wall on the side of Bonifraterska Street and the Powazki Cemetery.

Up till today, "Waclaw" does not know whether this message made it to the Ghetto at all, but it seems it did because Anielewicz was saying something about an expected attack and they even sent a boy there who did not make it (they burned him alive on Mila Street, the whole day one could hear him screaming), the moment Anielewicz got the message having been the sole time he seemed to regain any hope, even though everyone was telling him that it was impossible, that nobody would be able to force their way through there.

The burning boy was screaming on Mila Street, and meanwhile, on the other side of the wall, two guys lay on the street—they were supposed to have placed 50 kilograms of explosives at the Ghetto wall. The AK partisan, Zbigniew Mlynarski, who used the pseudonym "Kret," says that precisely this was the most horrible—that these two were killed at the very outset and that therefore nobody was going to get the explosives to the wall.

"The street was empty. The Germans were shooting at us from all over. The machine gun on the hospital roof that had been shooting into the Ghetto before was now shooting at us. Behind us, in Krasinski Square, an SS company was stationed, so that when Pszenny exploded that mine that was supposed to collapse the wall—instead, it went off in the street and mangled the bodies of our two guys. So we began to withdraw.

"Today," continues Mlynarski, "I know what we should have done: we should have entered the Ghetto, fired the explosives *inside*, and our people should have been waiting on the other side to lead the insurgents out.

"Only, when one thinks about it, how many of them would have still been there to leave? Not more than fifteen. And would even all of *them* have agreed to go?

"For them," continues Mlynarski, "there was this prestige aspect. Late, but in the end, they did commit themselves to make this painful sacrifice. And it's good that they did so because at least they preserved Jewish honor."

Exactly the same sort of comment is offered by Henryk Grabowski, in whose apartment Jurek Wilner used to hide arms and who later managed to spring Jurek from the clutches of the Gestapo:

"Those people did not want to live anymore anyway and one should consider it to their credit that they had the common sense to want to die in a battle. Because they were going to die in any case, so it's better to die with a weapon in one's hand than in some indecent manner."

Mr. Grabowski tells me how he came to understand this himself—how it is better to die putting up a fight—when he was stopped near the Ghetto one day as he was leaving, carrying a package of letters from Mordka Anielewicz. "Excuse me," Grabowski corrects himself, "I mean, from *Mordechaj*; one must be respectful of rank and position." They made him stand up against the wall, with a rifle barrel right in front of him, like this, at the level of this vase on the cabinet, and then he'd thought, "To at least be able to bite that Hun, to gouge his eyes out . . ." (Luckily, there had been a Polish policeman, a Mr. Wislocki, among the Germans, to whom he'd said: "All right, Mr. Wislocki, do your duty, but you should understand that I am not alone, so watch out that you don't have serious problems later on because of this . . ." Mr.

Wislocki had understood immediately, and they let him go at once.)

Mr. Grabowski had known Mordka for many years, since before the war. "He was, after all, one of us from down there, from the Powisle slum. We were in the same gang, we would always band together for brawls, or we'd go fight the boys from other districts like Wola or Gorny Mokotow."

There was the same sort of poverty at Mrs. Grabowski's as at Mrs. Anielewicz's. The one sold fish, the other bread, and if she sold ten loaves, forty bagels, and a few vegetables each day, that was it.

Already then, in Powisle, it was obvious that Mordka knew how to fight, so Mr. Grabowski wasn't all that surprised when he met him in the Ghetto, transformed into Mordechaj. On the contrary, it seemed to him quite natural: who, after all, should be the commander if not their guy from Powisle? (At that first meeting, Mordechaj told him what to convey to the boys in Wilno: that they should gather money, arms, and strong, committed young people.)

Mr. Grabowski had been a Boy Scout before the war, and all his friends from the older Scout troops had been executed in Palmiry within weeks of the Nazi invasion in 1939, all fifty of them. He'd survived and gotten an order from the Scout leadership to go to Wilno and organize Jews for the struggle.

In Wilno Kolonia, Mr. Grabowski met Jurek Wilner. There was a Dominican nunnery in Kolonia, and the Mother Superior was hiding a few Jews at her place. ("I told my sisters, 'Remember, Christ used to say that there is no greater love for God than when you give your life for your friends.' And they'd understood. . . .")

Jurek Wilner was the favorite of the Mother Superior— blond hair, blue eyes, he reminded her of her own brother who'd been taken away as a prisoner. So they often conversed: she would tell him about God, he would tell her about Marx. And when he was leaving for Warsaw, for the Ghetto, from which he would never return, he left her the most valuable thing he had: a notebook filled with poems. He would record in it the things he valued most and considered most important, and this notebook, in its brown plastic cover, its yellowed pages covered with Jurek's handwriting (it was she who had given him this name: Jurek had been Arie before), the Mother Superior has kept up till this day. "This book has come through a lot: a Gestapo visit, concentration camp, prison. Before I die I'd like to place it in some deserving hands."

From Jurek Wilner's notebook:

> *Don't look—don't—don't look—don't—*
> > *what's there ahead, before you*
> *(Shoes—shoes—shoes—shoes—up, down, up, down)*
> *People—people—people—people—*
> > *Obsessed with this vista*
> > *Well, there is no respite in war*
> *Try—think—think—think—about something prior,*
> > *something different*
> > *Oh my God—God—God—spare this mind*
> > *from madness!*
> *(Shoes—shoes—shoes—shoes—up, down, up, down)*
> > *There is no respite in war*
> *We—can—stand—hunger—cold—thirst—weariness*
> *But—not—not—not—not—not this continuous vista*
> *(Shoes—shoes—shoes—shoes—up, down, up, down)*
> *There is no respite in war.*

So Mr. Grabowski met Jurek in Wilno Kolonia, and when Jurek came to Warsaw, he moved in with Mr. Grabowski, on Podchorazych Street. All the Jews from Wilno arriving in Warsaw would first stay at Mr. Grabowski's, and he would immediately take them to the marketplace to buy them some adequate clothing. "Ski caps were very fashionable then, those caps with their little eye shades, but those boys didn't look good in them because in some odd way the eye shades accentuated their noses, so I would tell them, 'Bicycle caps, yes, hats, yes, but ski caps—absolutely under no condition!' " He also corrected their behavior, even the way they walked, so that they would move "without a Jewish accent."

Mr. Grabowski offered an interesting observation: the more afraid a person was, the uglier he became—his features would somehow become distorted. Those who were not afraid, on the other hand, fellows like Wilner and Anielewicz—they were really handsome guys and their faces really looked quite different.

As the ZOB's representative on the Aryan side (Mr. Grabowski would only learn later, after the war, the nature of his mission; in those days he preferred to know as little as possible, in order not to even be capable of spilling anything under interrogation), Jurek used to get in touch all the time with "Waclaw" and the officers, and when he was unable to take all the packets to the Ghetto, he would leave them at Mr. Grabowski's or with the barefoot Carmelite nuns on Wolska Street: sometimes guns, sometimes knives, or even explosives. At that time the barefoot Carmelite nuns did not have strictures as severe as those they observe today and they were allowed to show their faces to strangers, so Jurek, tired after carrying sacks, used to rest on a cot behind a screen in the locutory. I am sitting now in the same locutory on one side of a black iron bar, with the Mother Superior in a nook on the other side, at dusk, and we are talking about those arms transports for the Ghetto that went through the convent for almost a year. Didn't they have any misgivings? The Mother Superior does not understand . . .

"After all, arms in such a place?"

"You mean, perhaps, that arms serve to kill people?" asks the Mother Superior. No, for some reason she had never thought about it that way. Her only thought was for the fact that Jurek would eventually be making use of these arms and that when his last hour came, it would be good if he managed to make an act of contrition and make his peace with God. She even asked him to promise this to her, and now she asks me what I think; did he remember the promise when he shot himself in the bunker, at 18 Mila Street?

While Jurek and his friends were making use of those arms, the sky in this part of the town became quite red and this glow even reached into the convent's vestibule. That's why precisely there, and not in the chapel, the barefoot Carmelite nuns would gather each night and read psalms ("Yea, for Thy sake are we killed all the day long, we are counted as sheep for the slaughter. Awake! Why sleepest thou, oh Lord?"), and she prayed to God that Jurek Wilner might meet his death without fear.

So Jurek was gathering arms, and Mr. Grabowski, for his part, was busy helping him by complementing his purchases. Once, he managed to get a few hundred kilos of saltpeter and wood coal to make the explosives (he bought them from Stefan Oskroba, a drugstore owner at Narutowicz Square); another time, two hundred grams of cyanide the Jews wanted to have on themselves in case of arrest. The cyanide came in small blue-gray cubes, and Henryk first tested the stuff on a cat. He scratched off a little powder, sprinkled it over a piece of sausage, and the cat died at once—so that Henryk could give it to Wilner without any compunctions. Because Henryk, as the owner of a bacon and meat stand, had his peddler's honor and couldn't sell bad merchandise to a friend.

Henryk "Baconman"—because this was Mr. Grabowski's pseudonym—and Jurek Wilner were very close friends. When they slept on the same pallet (Henryk's wife and daughter slept on the bed, under which were stored the packs of knives and grenades), they would talk about everything. That it had turned cold, how they were hungry, that killings were going on all around, and how it would soon be necessary to risk their own heads. "As far as his intellect went," remembers Henryk, "Jurek had a philosophical mind, so we often spoke about what the point of it all was, and he had such a humanistic attitude toward life in general."

From Jurek Wilner's notebook:

And in a day—
           we'll not meet each other anymore
And in a week—
           we'll not greet each other anymore
And in a month—
           we'll have forgotten each other
And in a year
           we won't even recognize each other
And today the night over this black river
is like a coffin lid
which I try to pry open with my scream:
Listen—save me!
Listen—I love you!
Can you hear me?—
           It's already too far.

During the first days of March 1943 Jurek Wilner was arrested by the Gestapo.

"The morning of that day," says attorney Wolinski, "I'd been at his place in Wspolna Street, and around two in the afternoon the Germans surrounded the building and took him with his documents and arms.

"We had an unwritten law that if someone got arrested, he had to keep silent for at least three days. After that, if he was broken, nobody would blame him for that. They tortured Jurek Wilner for a month, and he gave not a thing away—no contacts, no addresses, although he knew plenty of them, both on the Jewish side and on the Aryan side as well.

"He escaped by a miracle, at the end of March, but he went back to the Ghetto, and he was useless after that for any work: his feet were smashed and he couldn't walk."

The miraculous escape attorney Wolinski speaks about had been arranged for Jurek by his friend Henryk "Baconman." He found out that Jurek was being kept in a camp in the Grochow district, he sneaked in through the swamps, got him out, and took him home.

Jurek's nails, kidneys, and feet were all smashed, he had been tortured every day, and one day he'd joined a group destined for execution, hoping that this would end it all faster. It turned out that the group was being taken to a work camp in Grochow instead, and that was where Mr. Grabowski found him.

Everybody set to caring for him—Mr. Grabowski, his mother, his wife, they would rub his nails with something (these nails were just peeling off his fingers), they gave him pills after which he would pee blue. Finally Jurek got better and said he wanted to go back to the Ghetto. Mr. Grabowski told him: "Jurek, what do you need that for? I'll take you to the country. . . ." But Jurek said he had to go back. To which Mr. Grabowski replied: "You'll see, I can hide you real well, nobody will find you till the end of the war. . . ."

They didn't even say good-bye to each other. When his friends came to pick Jurek up, Henryk happened to be out. And after the Ghetto uprising broke out, Henryk understood immediately that this would be the end for Jurek—that from this adventure he was certainly not destined to escape. Not the adventure, of course, but the tragedy that was about to transpire.

And indeed, Jurek did not escape—and from one of the last ZOB reports, we learn that it was precisely he who called for suicide on May 8th in the bunker at 18 Mila Street.

"Because of the hopeless situation and to avoid falling into the Germans' hands alive, Arie Wilner called on the fighters to commit suicide. As the first one, Lutek Rotblat initially shot his mother and then himself. In the bunker most of the members of the Combat Organization found their deaths, including Commander Mordechaj Anielewicz."

After the war Henryk (he initially had a repair garage, then a taxi cab, and then he worked in transportation, as a clerk in the technical department) often pondered whether he'd done the right thing letting Jurek go. In the country he would certainly have been cured, become stronger . . . "But, on the other hand, had he survived, perhaps he would have been angry with me? He would certainly have been angry to be alive, and it would have been even worse. . . ."

From Jurek Wilner's notebook:

So once again a little more
why does someone always have to spoil it for me,
to cut the halter?
Yesterday I could already feel death in my bones
Had eternity complete
inside.
They handed me a spoon,
a spoonful of life.
I didn't want it, I don't want this drink:
Let me throw it up.
I know life is a full pot
and that the world is good and healthy,
but life doesn't make it into my blood,
it only gives me cerebral congestion.
It feeds others, but it saps me . . .

"I wrote a letter to him in the Ghetto," says "Waclaw" (attorney Wolinski). "I don't remember exactly what I wrote, but they were tender words, the kind it is so difficult to write.

"His death was very painful to me. The death of every single one of those men was painful to me.

"Such honorable men.

"So heroic.

"So Polish."

After Jurek Wilner's arrest in March, Antek became the ZOB's representative on the Aryan side.

"He was a very nice and brave man," says attorney Wolinski. "Only he had a horrible habit: he always carried a bag full of grenades around with him. It made me a bit nervous because I always thought they would explode."

One of the first telegrams "Waclaw" had sent to London concerned money. Those under his charge needed it for arms, and at first, $5000 arrived in the drops.

"I gave it to Mikolaj from the 'Bund,' and all of a sudden Borowski, a Zionist, came to me with a complaint. 'Mr. Waclaw,' he said, 'he took everything and doesn't want to give any of it to me, please tell him something.'"

But Mikolaj by that time had already given the money to Edelman, and Edelman had given it to Tosia, and Tosia had hidden it under a polishing broom, and, as they were soon to experience, this was a brilliant idea, because during a search the whole apartment was ransacked, but it hadn't occurred to anybody to look under the floor polisher. With this money they were later able to buy some arms on the Aryan side.

Tosia subsequently ransomed "Waclaw" from the Gestapo: someone sent her a message that he had been arrested, and she immediately thought, "Who knows, maybe something can be arranged with a Persian rug." And indeed, thanks to the rug, "Waclaw" got out. "Why, yes," says Tosia, "it was really a beautiful rug. One of those beige ones, with selvage around the border and a medallion in the center."

Tosia—Dr. Teodozja Goliborska—the last of the doctors who participated in the research on hunger in the Ghetto—has come from Australia to visit for a few days, so there are many people today at attorney Wolinski's house. There is a lot of social animation, a hum, and everybody is competing at telling funny stories. For example, all the problems "Waclaw" had with those people from the ZOB who were always liquidating the Nazi collaborators too quickly. The sentence was supposed to come first and then the execution, but they'd come up to him and say: "Mr. Waclaw, we've already taken care of him." "And what was I supposed to do? I had to write to the executions committee to arrange for a post-facto formal sentence."

Or, perhaps, the story of what happened with that big drop. One hundred and twenty thousand dollars arrived and. . . . "Just a second," says Edelman. "Was it one hundred and twenty thousand dollars? We got only half of that."

"Mr. Marek," says Waclaw, "you guys got it all and you bought guns with it."

"Those fifty guns?"

"Of course not. Those fifty guns you didn't buy, those you got from us, from the Home Army. Well, actually not quite all of them, because one of them was sent to Czestochowa and that Jew used it, you remember? And twenty of them were sent to Poniatow . . ."

So everybody is chatting like this, and Tosia also recalls the red sweater Marek was wearing as he ran along the rooftops. She says that it was a real *shmate* compared to the sweater she will immediately send him as soon as she gets back to Australia. And now, when we are already on our way home, Edelman suddenly turns to me and says: "It wasn't a month. It was a few days, a week at most."

He's talking about Jurek Wilner. That he withstood a week and not a month of torture at the hands of the Gestapo.

Now, just a second. "Waclaw" spoke about one month, Mr. Grabowski about two weeks . . .

"I remember precisely that he was there for one week."

This is beginning to get annoying.

If "Waclaw" said it was a month, he must have known what he was talking about.

But what does it come down to? That all of us want very much for Jurek Wilner to have withstood the Gestapo tortures for as long as possible. It is, after all, a big difference: to maintain that silence for a week as opposed to a month. Really, we very much want Jurek Wilner to have held his tongue for the whole month.

"All right," he says, "Antek wants us to have been five hundred, that writer Mr. S. wants the mother to have been the one who painted the fish, and you all want him to have been in prison for a month. So let it be a month. After all, it doesn't matter at this point."

It is the same with the banners.

They'd been hanging over the Ghetto from the first day of the uprising: white and red, and blue and white. They provoked an outpouring of affection on the Aryan side, and the Germans finally took them down, with the greatest difficulty and the greatest satisfaction, as war trophies.

He says that if there were any banners there, it could only have been his people who hung them, and his people had not hung any banners. They would have liked to hang them, if they had had some white and red fabric, but they hadn't.

"Perhaps somebody else hung them, it doesn't matter who."

"Oh, yes," he says. "Possibly." Only, he didn't see any banners at all. He only learned about them after the war.

"That's impossible. Everybody saw them!"

"Well, if everybody saw them, they must have been there, these banners. And besides," he says, "what does it matter? All that's important is that people saw them."

This is the worst part: that in the end he agrees to everything. And it doesn't even make any sense to try to convince him.

"What difference does it make today?" he asks, and then he agrees.

We have to write about one more thing," he says.

Why he is alive.

When the first soldier of the liberating army came in, he stopped him and asked, "You're Jewish—so how come you're alive?" The question seemed laced with suspicion: perhaps he'd turned somebody in? Perhaps he'd taken somebody else's bread? So I should ask him now whether by chance he didn't survive on somebody else's account, and if not, then why he actually did survive.

And then he will try to explain himself. For instance, he will tell me about the day he went to Nowolipki Street, number seven, where their conspiracy had a local safehouse, to tell somebody that Irka, a woman doctor from the Leszno hospital, was lying unconscious in an apartment across the street. When the entire hospital was being taken to the Umschlagplatz, Irka had swallowed a bottle of Luminal, put on a nightgown, and gone to bed. He'd found her in this pink gown and brought her to a house where everybody else had already been taken away, and now he wanted to tell the others that if she was to survive, it would be necessary to get her out of there.

There was a wall just across the street at Nowolipki Street—on the other side it was already the Aryan part. All of a sudden an SS man leaned out from behind that wall and started shooting. He shot more than fifteen times—each time, less than half a meter to his right. Perhaps the SS man was astigmatic—it is the sort of visual defect that can be corrected by glasses, but the German apparently had an uncorrected astigmatism, so he missed.

"Is that all?" I ask. "Simply that the German soldier didn't have the right glasses?"

But there comes another story, this one about Mietek Dab.

One day, the contingent of people in the Umschlagplatz was a little short of the required ten thousand, and some people, Edelman included, were simply gathered up from a nearby street, piled onto a platform cart, and transported down to Stawki Street toward the Umschlagplatz. The cart was being pulled by two horses; a Jewish policeman was sitting next to the driver and there was a German at the back.

They were already passing Nowolipki Street when Marek suddenly noticed Mietek Dab walking down the street. He was a member of the Socialist Party, he had been assigned to serve in the Ghetto police, he happened to live on Nowolipki Street, and he was heading home from work.

"Mietek, I got caught," Marek yelled, and Mietek came running up close, told the policeman that he was his brother, and they let him off the cart.

Then they went to Mietek's house.

Mietek's father was there—short, thin, hungry. He looked at them with distaste:

"Mietek managed to save somebody from the cart again, right? And as usual, he didn't take a penny for it?

"He could have made thousands already.

"He might at least have been able to buy some rationed bread with the money.

"But what does he do? He gets people off for free."

"Daddy," said Mietek, "don't worry. It will count to my credit as an act of kindness and I'll go to heaven."

"What heaven? What God!? Can't you see what's going on? Don't you see that there hasn't been any God for a long time? And even if there is," the little old man lowered his voice, *"He is on THEIR side."*

The next day they took Mietek's dad. Mietek didn't get back in time to get him off the cart, and soon thereafter, Mietek escaped into the forest, to join the partisans.

This is the second example: when he should have died for certain, and again some coincidence saved him. In the first case, he was saved by the SS man's astigmatism; in the second, by the fact that Mietek Dab happened to be walking down the street on his way home from work.

Those girls brought in with pink sputum foaming on their lips (the ones who'd still manage to grow up and make love and have babies, that is, still manage so much more than Mrs. Tenenbaum's daughter ever managed to do), they were often suffering from narrowed valves. Valves are somewhat like rhythmically moving petals that allow the blood to flow through. When they are narrowed, not enough blood flows and lung edema can occur—the heart begins to work faster in order to transmit more blood, but it can only beat so fast, because the ventricles need time to fill with blood. . . . The optimum workload is four thousand two hundred heartbeats per hour, more than a hundred thousand a day, during which time the heart pumps seven thousand liters of blood, which is to say, five tons! I know all this from Sejdak the engineer, who says that a heart is just a machine like any other machine and, like all machines, has certain specific properties: it has big reserves of efficiency, and the use of material is low because it is able to regenerate used parts, in other words, to renovate itself day by day.

When the heart is not able to conduct its self-renovation properly, it begins to fall sick. And most often it is precisely the heart's valves that begin to break down first, which is actually quite understandable, says Sejdak the engineer, because they are precisely valves, and in any machine it's the valves that break first—take, for instance, your car.

Understanding the essence of a heart's work was therefore not that difficult for Sejdak the engineer, thanks to which in a year and a half he managed to build a machine for the Professor that could temporarily replace the real heart during its repair, which is to say, its surgery.

The cost of this mechanical heart was four hundred thousand zlotys. It was a unique, world-class invention for which Sejdak the engineer procured a patent, but when the work was finally completed, an inspector came to the Merinotex plant and found out that these accounting costs had not been recorded in the column where they should have been, which meant that Sejdak the engineer had caused losses for the factory, which in turn meant that he had committed an economic crime.

Luckily, Sejdak the engineer managed to pull together the necessary official documentation forms, and he was acquitted of this charge of transgression; the inspector was even kind enough not to include mention of the case in his report.

Sejdak is currently working on a new machine. It will help the heart pump blood through narrowed valves, and it will make it possible for patients to survive the time between a heart attack and the subsequent surgery. Most people in this situation die almost immediately after the heart attack and don't even make it to the operation. If this machine really turns out to work, it should save the lives of many people, or at least (says Edelman) it may shield the flame for one more moment.

One obviously shouldn't exaggerate this hope. After all, He is looking on very carefully both at Sejdak and at the Professor and at all these efforts of theirs, and He is always capable of striking in the most unexpected ways. For instance, they all imagined that everything had gone well, that they were all home free, and Stefan, Marysia Sawicka's brother, was maybe the happiest of them all because he was just seventeen and he had been given his first gun. Marysia Sawicka was the one who before the war used to run the eight hundred meters with Michal Klepfisz's sister in the Skra club. So Stefan was seventeen and he had his first weapon and his happiness at having taken part in an action (he'd been in the group safeguarding their removal from the sewers) was almost making him burst. He was unable to stay put at home, and he'd run downstairs to the confectionery, and at precisely that moment a German soldier just happened to enter the shop and notice the gun in Stefan's pocket; he simply took him outside and killed him on the spot, in front of the building, right beneath Marysia's windows.

Sometimes it is a real race, and right up till the very end, He does not spare you His petty, small-minded nastinesses. Take the Rudny case, where He seemed to be busy scrambling up everything: the coronography doctor was missing, the light bulb in the X-ray unit went out, the operating room was locked up, the scrub nurses weren't around. . . . All the while, Rudny's pain was increasing, each stab of pain might have been his last, and they were all still looking for cars, doctors, bulbs, and nurses. But that time they made it. At 3 A.M. as they were thanking the Professor, and the Professor was thanking them, as blood was already flowing through the wider channels in Rudny's veins and his heart was once again working normally—they had to agree that this time they'd succeeded, they'd succeeded once more.

Before Rudny's surgery Edelman hadn't been quite sure if it was going to be possible to operate in an acute state such as this because he had read in all the books how one shouldn't, and he left the hospital to think it over one more time in calm. He'd run into Dr. Zadrozna, and he'd asked her: "Should we operate? What do you think?" and Dr. Zadrozna had been very surprised. "What?" she'd said, "in *your* situation?" Because at the time they had been having some minor problems at work, or actually he had been, because he'd gotten fired and Elzbieta Chetkowska and Aga Zuchowska had decided to resign in solidarity with him—some insignificant matter, but serious enough so that Dr. Zadrozna could be surprised, since an unsuccessful operation would not have made it any easier for them to find new jobs. But the minute he'd heard "What? . . ." he'd immediately realized that there was nothing more to think about, the decision was made, and was even made in a way without him. So he went back to the hospital and announced, "We are operating," and Elzbieta trounced him for even having gone out at all when he knew so well how much every minute counted.

Or, for instance, a patient is brought in, and everybody says that she is suffering from catatonia, a version of schizophrenia where the afflicted patient doesn't eat or move, just sleeps, and it is impossible to wake her up. She has been treated for catatonia for fifteen years. While she is still asleep, they do a blood test, and it turns out that she registers at more than 30 milligrams of sugar, and it suddenly occurs to everyone that this isn't schizophrenia at all, but rather some dysfunction of the pancreas. They operate on the pancreas and then the biggest tension starts: immediately after the operation, she's up at 130 milligrams of sugar, a bit too much;

after two hours—60, a bit too little—everyone gets nervous that the count is decreasing too fast; but after another four hours, it's still 60, so perhaps things have stabilized after all.

The pancreas problem ends. Everyday life resumes, but then a patient suffering from kidney disease arrives with a mysterious upsurge in his calcium. So it becomes necessary to ask one's colleagues what the clinical symptoms of an overacute parathyroid are, and obviously nobody knows because this sort of thing only happens once every few years. They call Paris, to the calcium experts at Professor Royuxe's center, who tell them to send a hormone sample for testing in a container chilled to minus thirty-two degrees Celsius, but the patient's calcium count has already reached sixteen and one dies at twenty, so they rush him for surgery to Warsaw, perhaps the count will remain stable during the transit; only exactly at the moment he is being put on the operating table, his count reaches twenty, and the patient fades. . . .

The parathyroid problem ends. Everyday life resumes.

I mention all this to Zbigniew Mlynarski—pseudonym "Mole"—the one who was getting ready to blow up the wall on Bonifraterska Street. He'd been aiming his gun at exactly the same moment that, on the other side of the wall, at Edelman's, they'd exploded that single mine of theirs. (Mlynarski had been aiming at a German cop who was aiming at him: luckily Mlynarski was better by a fraction of a second.) So I ask Mlynarski whether he understands all this about Edelman, and he says he understands, he understands it very well. He himself, for example, after the war became chairman of a fur makers' cooperative. He remembers that period very well because he had to act quickly and make risky decisions. For instance, once he used the cooperative's floating capital to repair the roof. Rain was flooding the furs. But he got into trouble, was threatened with prosecution. He said, "All right, take me to court. So I spent two million without any formal clearance. I saved thirty." It ended up that nobody did anything to him, but that decision had really required courage: to use the floating capital in those years for a roof. And that's exactly what matters in life, Mlynarski concludes: the ability to make quick, manly decisions.

After the cooperative, Mlynarski had a private shop making furs for state-owned companies. He employed four workers and had no more problems with the finance department. One of the workers would stretch the skins, the second would cut them, the third one would measure them out, and the fourth one would finish up. He himself had the most responsible job: matching them together—because the most important thing in the fur maker's profession is to make one skin match another.

But actually it was only during the war that Mlynarski lived a full life: "I am insignificant as a man—60 kilos and 163 centimeters—and yet back in those days I was braver than all those guys over 180." Later he put together the material to make skins match. "Can one take it seriously?" he asks. "After all that—ending up matching astrakhan furs?" That's why he understands Dr. Edelman so well.

The only thing that matters is to shield the flame.

But, as we have said, He sits above, carefully observing all these efforts, and is capable of lashing out so suddenly that it is then too late to do a thing: they test her blood and it turns out that it is glutethimide, and nothing can be done anymore. Why did she take glutethimide? Or with this other one: it might have been a hematoma at the back of her skull. She was confusing words, couldn't remember the easiest symbols, she'd forget an address now and then or how to turn a light on, things like that. . . . She had everything—loving parents, a room with expensive toys, and later a wonderful degree and a handsome fiancé, but one day she swallowed sleeping pills and all that remains is that beautiful room, willow green and white, where her good American father doesn't let anyone move even a single thing and says it will remain like this forever. The American father asked Dr. Edelman why she'd done it, but he was unable to answer, even though it was Elzunia, the daughter of Zygmunt, the one who had said: "I will not survive but you will, so remember that in Zamosc, in a convent, there is a child. . . ." Later, Zygmunt shot into the searchlight, thanks to which they managed to jump the wall, and immediately after the war Edelman found Elzunia. He wasn't able to help either of them: Elzunia who died in New York, or the other woman who died here. . . .

So you never know who's outsmarted whom. Sometimes you are happy that you've succeeded, you have checked everything thoroughly and you know that nothing bad should happen anymore, and then Stefan, Marysia's brother, dies because he was overwhelmed with happiness, or Celina, the one who got out with them through the sewers on Prosta Street, lies dying and all he can promise her is that she will die in a dignified manner and without fear.

(Edelman later went to Celina's funeral and there were three of them there from that sewer on Prosta Street: he, Masza, and Pnina. And Masza, the moment she noticed him, whispered: "You know, I heard him again today." "Whom?" he asked. "Don't try to pretend that you don't know," she got angry. He was later told that Masza kept hearing the scream of that boy who'd gone to find out what the message "Wait in the northern part of the Ghetto" meant. They burned him on Mila Street and he screamed the whole day; and Masza, who spent that day in a nearby bunker, today, in Jerusalem, a town three thousand kilometers away from Mila Street and from that bunker, lurks and waits for Pnina to go shopping and then whispers: "Listen, I heard him again today. Very clearly.")

Or, the super knocks at the door of Abrasza Blum's land-

116

lady, hisses, "There is a Jew in your apartment," locks the door, and goes to the telephone (the Home Army later sentenced this super to death, Abrasza jumped out the window to a roof, he broke his legs and lay crumpled like that until the Gestapo came); or a patient dies on the operating table because it was a circumferential infarction, which gave no picture on either the coronography or the EKG. So you well remember all these tricks and even when the operation seems to end, well—you wait.

There will be long days of waiting, because only gradually will it be revealed whether the heart will adapt to the patched-up veins, to the new aortas, and to the medication. Later, gradually, you get calmer, you become more confident. . . . And as this tension and later this happiness gradually leave you, only then do you finally realize the proportion: one to four hundred thousand.

1:400,000.

It is simply ludicrous.

But every life is a full one hundred percent for each individual, so that perhaps it makes some sense after all.

TRANSLATORS' AFTERWORD

In his essay introducing this volume, Timothy Garton Ash describes the remarkable impact of Hanna Krall's interview with Marek Edelman when it first burst on the Polish literary scene in the mid-1970s. He suggests the way in which Polish and Jewish histories—for so many centuries so intimately interwoven, in so many ways so ironically similar—had virtually bifurcated in the decades since the war, so that in recent years the two histories tended to haunt each other without any real lived, experienced interpenetration. In many ways—to take just one side of that bifurcation—Jews had become like ghosts for most Poles: phantasms, bogeymen for some, for most (especially for the young) hardly more than rumors. And yet, as late as 1939, more than three million Jews made up almost 10 percent of Poland's total population (30 percent of Warsaw's, over 50 percent in several other major towns). Of course, the vast majority of Poland's Jews perished during the Nazi Holocaust of the next several years, and most of those who survived left the country in the years immediately thereafter, settling for the most part in either America or Israel. Still, tens of thousands remained, and many of them rose to positions of considerable professional, bureaucratic, and academic prominence during the 1950s and 1960s. Then, in 1968, a power struggle inside the Polish Communist Party featured a virulent upwelling of anti-Semitic pressures and propaganda: tens of thousands of Polish Jews were purged from their positions and ended up leaving the country. Many of the people who today occupy positions of commanding prominence in Poland benefited decisively from the opportunities afforded them, earlier in their careers, during those 1968 purges: they simply leapfrogged into the vacancies created by the departed Jews, and have been rising ever since. Still, some Jews remained in Poland even after the 1968 purges, and two in particular were the cardiologist from Lodz, Marek Edelman, and the young Warsaw journalist Hanna Krall. And the meteoric success of the book they were to fashion together less than a decade later suggested that a new generation of Poles was in fact intensely curious about that ghost history, the fate of the country's Jews—indeed, that it might be time for the emergence of a *common* history of Poles and Jews. These early indications were to receive confirmation and amplification in the years immediately thereafter.

One of the most important legacies of the sixteen months of Solidarity's above-ground existence, from August 1980 through the imposition of martial law in December 1981, was the way in which the buried issue of Polish-Jewish relations was uncovered, ventilated, and in a significant way confronted and reclaimed through the self-conscious exertions of the union. Several of Solidarity's leading theorists were Jewish—notably Adam Michnik and Karol Modzelewski—as were many of the movement's most eloquent chroniclers. Hanna Krall was herself responsible for producing one of the period's most influential texts, a wonderfully moving interview with Anna Walentynowicz, the humble, much-beloved crane operator in the Gdansk shipyards whose firing had sparked the August strike. And Marek Edelman, for his part, was rediscovered as a *Polish* hero for his contributions in the common anti-Nazi effort. He became an important Solidarity figure in his native Lodz and was indeed elected as a regional delegate to the union's first (and last) annual national congress in Gdansk in September 1981. There, one veteran of the Home Army interrupted the congress's celebration of his own exploits to insist that the convention had in its midst a hero of considerably greater stature, Dr. Marek Edelman over in the Lodz delegation. The congress rose in ovation.

Throughout this period, Solidarity's theorists and spokesmen repeatedly advanced a new conception of Polish history and nationhood, one that integrated the contributions of minorities who had previously existed unassimilated and even been actively discriminated against. The enormously respected historian Jan Jozef Lipski, one of the principal architects of K.O.R. (the Committee for the Defense of the Workers, a precursor of Solidarity active in the years after 1976), composed an influential essay entitled "Two Fatherlands, Two Patriotisms," in which he offered a devastating critique of the xenophobic tendencies in prior Polish culture, which, he argued, would have to be overcome if the nation were ever to achieve a true and just sovereignty. Over and over again, Solidarity spokesmen warned their members to be on guard against divisive anti-Semitic tactics; they demonstrated how throughout Polish history, ruling elites (be they Russians or Germans or even native Poles) had succeeded in dividing natural allies from one another through the exploitation of this canard of anti-Semitism, thereby facilitating their subjugation of the nation. And this process of mass consciousness-raising appears in large measure to have worked, for when the shadowy, para-official Grunwald Patriotic Association launched a dark campaign of anti-Semitic innuendo during the spring of 1981, aimed at discrediting Solidarity's leadership, virtually no one rose to the bait.

After the December 1981 imposition of martial law, the

Polish regime doubled back, reined in the anti-Semitic innuendoes of its minions, and tried to garner a measure of international legitimacy by announcing plans for a massive celebration of the upcoming fortieth anniversary of the Warsaw Ghetto uprising in April 1983. As the last survivor of the Ghetto uprising's command group living anywhere in the world,* Marek Edelman was invited to sit on the committee presiding over arrangements for the observances. But in an open letter, dated February 2, 1983, he emphatically refused the invitation:

> *Forty years ago we fought not only for our lives. We fought for life in dignity and freedom. To celebrate our anniversary here where social life is dominated throughout by humiliation and coercion would be to deny our fight. It would mean participating in something contrary to its ideals. It would be an act of cynicism and contempt. I shall not participate in such arrangements or accept the participation of others who do so, regardless of where they come from or whom they represent. Far from these manipulated celebrations, in the silence of the graves and in people's hearts, there shall live the true memory of the victims and the heroes, the memory of the eternal human striving for freedom and truth.*

The regime nevertheless went ahead with the commemoration. A couple of days before the official event, on April 17, several hundred Solidarity members staged a commemoration of their own, gathering spontaneously at the Warsaw Ghetto Memorial. (Lech Walesa was detained by police in

---

*At the time Hanna Krall's text was first published in Poland, another surviving ZOB command group leader—Anielewicz's deputy, Itzhak Zuckermann, also known as "Antek"—was still living in Israel, although he had not actually been in the Ghetto at the time of the uprising. In any case, he had died in the meantime.

Gdansk as he was getting into a car to make the journey down, so he was prevented from attending.) Janusz Onyszkiewicz, one of the former union's official press spokesmen, who'd only just been released from detention three months earlier, read a statement in which he insisted, among other things, that Solidarity had fought for some of the same ideals as had the insurgents of the Warsaw Ghetto—whereupon he was promptly rearrested. A statement from Marek Edelman was also read out: the doctor explained that he was unfortunately prevented from being present at this occasion because he was being held under house arrest back in Lodz.

Which, indeed, he was—"for his own protection" was the way the regime's spokesmen attempted to rationalize the situation. But he was not entirely alone: Hanna Krall had come down from Warsaw for the day. And several months later, as we were translating this book, Ms. Krall returned to that afternoon in a letter she wrote us about how her narrative might be "brought up to date":

I think that we should consider some of the contemporary things. You know, there was throughout this book a loneliness, the loneliness of a man behind the walls, a man who wasn't even sure whether the world would hear them shooting. The loneliness of a man who felt he had a face from the poster "Jews—Lice— Typhoid" among all those fair and beautiful people (do you remember this little scene in the book when he takes a streetcar for the first time after the uprising and wishes he didn't have a face?). In fact, throughout the 37 years following the war and up through our conversations, he felt lonely and unwanted and only in 1980 did it turn out that somebody needed him ("Solidarity needed him as a hero"). Finally somebody wanted him! This is where his blind love for Solidarity comes from. I think he was looking in Solidarity for the same things he'd experienced in the ZOB—the closeness, the fraternity, all those fundamental things. His decision not to participate in the official commem-

123

oration in 1983 seemed to me at first dubious; I felt that over those ashes there should be a moment of silence amidst all that political noise. But after everything that happened on April 17th, the rally and Onyszkiewicz's speech and all—I understood for the first time that the Ghetto uprising had now become a Polish thing. Because the truth is there had always been the main road of the Polish resistance movement, and alongside it there had run this honored though seldom-used path (because who would ever travel it?) of the fight of Jews. Thanks to the commemoration organized by Solidarity about which everybody soon knew, thanks to Edelman, and thanks to the regime, which precisely on the 40th anniversary of the uprising greeted its leader with a house-arrest, this Jewish path became for a while part of this whole, Polish war story. And when Edelman was sitting in his house surrounded by the police cars, sitting at a table set for a fancy dinner which included many empty places because the police were not letting the guests in (for some reason they'd let me by), a table where there were in any case more ghosts than live people— well, when Edelman was spending this day cut off from the world, not even for a moment did he have the feeling that he was alone. On the contrary, he had the feeling of belonging to the world, to that world of fair and brave people, and beautiful, and calm.

—Joanna Stasinska
Lawrence Weschler